PRICES, PROFITS AND FINANCIAL STRUCTURES

NEW DIRECTIONS IN MODERN ECONOMICS
Series Editor: Malcolm C. Sawyer, Professor of Economics,
University of Leeds

New Directions in Modern Economics presents a challenge to
orthodox economic thinking. It focuses on new ideas emanating
from radical traditions including post-Keynesian, Kaleckian,
neo-Ricardian and Marxian. The books in the series do not adhere
rigidly to any single school of thought but share in common an
attempt to present a positive alternative to the conventional
wisdom.

The main emphasis of the series is on the development and
application of new ideas to current problems in economic theory
and economic policy. It will include new original contributions to
theory, overviews of work in the radical tradition and the
evaluation of alternative economic policies. Some books will be
monographs whilst others will be suitable for adoption as texts.
The series will highlight theoretical and policy issues common to
all modern economies and is designed to appeal to economists
throughout the world regardless of their country of origin.

Published titles:

Post Keynesian Monetary Economics
New Approaches to Financial Modelling
Edited by Philip Arestis

Keynes's Principle of Effective Demand
Edward J. Amadeo

New Directions in Post-Keynesian Economics
Edited by John Pheby

Theory and Policy in Political Economy
Essays in Pricing, Distribution and Growth
Edited by Philip Arestis and Yiannis Kitromilides

Keynes's Third Alternative?
The Neo-Ricardian Keynesians and the Post Keynesians
Edward J. Amadeo and Amitava K. Dutt

Wages and Profits in the Capitalist Economy
The Impact of Monopolistic Power on Macroeconomic
Performance in the USA and UK
Andrew Henley

PRICES, PROFITS AND FINANCIAL STRUCTURES

A Post-Keynesian Approach to Competition

GÖKHAN ÇAPOĞLU

Associate Professor of Economics
Bilkent University, Turkey

Edward Elgar

Published by
Edward Elgar Publishing Limited
Gower House
Croft Road
Aldershot
Hants GU11 3HR
England

Edward Elgar Publishing Company
Old Post Road
Brookfield
Vermont 05036
USA

British Library Cataloguing in Publication Data
Çapoğlu, Gökhan
  Prices, profits and financial structures. – (New directions in modern economics).
  1. Investment
  I. Title   II. Series
  332.6

Library of Congress Cataloguing in Publication Data
Çapoğlu, Gökhan, 1956–
  Prices, profits, and financial structures: a post-Keynesian approach to competition/Gökhan Çapoğlu.
     p.   cm. – (New directions in modern economics series)
     Includes bibliographical references and indexes.
     1. Competition. 2. Prices. 3. Profit. I. Title. II. Series.
HB238.C37 1991   91–2510
338.5–dc20   CIP

ISBN 1 85278 410 5

Printed and bound in Great Britain by Billing & Sons Ltd, Worcester

Contents

Tables

Preface

This book is an expanded and revised version of my Ph.D. dissertation submitted to the Economics Department of the University of California, Berkeley. From the very beginning of my graduate study at Berkeley, I was distressed with the way neoclassicals analyse economic problems. I found the neoclassical approach assuming away the very problems that are supposed to be analysed, distorting the basic concepts of economic theory to facilitate technical analysis. For example, the assumption of perfect capital mobility eliminates the basic source of economic problems. Whenever neoclassicals talk about uncertainty, they turn to the risk apparatus which negates uncertainty. Historical time is abandoned for the technically manageable analytical time. The concept of competition is stripped of its behavioural content and defined as a market structure, paving the way for the equilibrium framework. The role of profits and technological change become unimportant in this static approach. Institutions simply do not matter.

While questioning the role of profits and technological change in capitalist economies, I found that the conception of competition is central in addressing these issues. The conception of competition as a survival process explains the role of profits and technological change in capitalist economies. Uncertainty is an integral part of technological change and the investment process. History and institutions do matter in the survival process. Thus, the equilibrium analysis becomes meaningless.

This book develops the concept of competition as a survival process, operationalizes it in a post-Keynesian model, and tests it econometrically. This is an area relatively undeveloped in the post-Keynesian approach. I hope that this book will attract the attention of post-Keynesians to the central role of the concept of competition in economic theory.

Writing a book is a collective effort stimulated by earlier contributions as acknowledged in the references section. However, some people were personally involved in this process whom I would like to thank by name. First, I am grateful to Professors Benjamin Ward, Laura D'Andrea Tyson and Richard Walker of Berkeley for giving me the opportunity to work with them on a topic I firmly believe in. I would also like to thank Professors Clair Brown and Jack Letiche and my classmate Allen Cheadle at Berkeley for their support at various stages of the dissertation.

One of the most pleasant and fruitful aspects of writing this book has been to meet very nice people and post-Keynesian colleagues. Professor John Pheby of Leicester Polytechnic was very kind to recommend my book to Mr Edward Elgar. I have benefited greatly from the comments of my series editor, Professor Malcolm Sawyer of the University of Leeds. Professor Philip Arestis of the Polytechnic of East London provided valuable comments on the final draft of the manuscript. I would like to thank them all.

I would also like to thank Mr Edward Elgar, my publisher, who was very helpful and efficient throughout this process and Ms. Julie Leppard.

It is to my wife, Toni, that I owe my greatest thanks for her unfailing support in all ways from the very beginning of this endeavour. In dedicating this book to her I simply express my deep gratitude and love.

1. Introduction

THE SETTING

Empirical evidence shows that firms in the United States finance their investment expenditures (I) mostly through their internal funds (IF, defined as undistributed profits plus capital consumption allowances). Internal financing ratios of investment expenditures (IF/I) not only change across industries in a given country but also between countries, as shown in tables 1.1 and 1.2.

In Table 1.1 the data are divided into two periods to show the general decline in the internal funds/investment ratio in the more recent period. However, the fact that there are significant differences in the internal funds/investment ratios across industries is clear in both periods. As Table 1.2 shows, firms in the United States and Britain finance themselves through their internal funds. The ratio of internal financing is close to 90 per cent in the United States and Britain, whereas it stays between 60–70 per cent in other countries.

The fact that US firms finance their investment expenditures largely through their internal funds, though observed by earlier writers,[1] has not been incorporated into economic theory. Incorporation of these facts into economic theory requires a joint analysis of firms' pricing, investment and financing decisions which are conventionally analysed under three separate subfields in economic theory. The theory of the firm concentrates exclusively on the determination of price under different market structures without taking into account firms' investment decisions and sources of finance. The only difference between dynamics and statics in such pricing models is that, in the former case, firms maximize the dis-

1

counted value of profits rather than profits themselves. There is no incorporation of investment behaviour into pricing decisions. Theories of investment, on the other hand, take no account of pricing behaviour because they assume perfect competition in which firms are price takers (Jorgenson 1963). Finally, the financial literature takes the price and investment decisions of firms as given, then analyses the composition of external financing (i.e. the mix of debt and equity) rather than the composition of internal versus external financing (Modigliani and Miller 1958). More importantly, the independence of real investment decisions from financing decisions forms the cornerstone of the Modigliani–Miller theory of finance. It would make more sense if these three decisions, crucial for

Table 1.1   Internal funds[1]/investment[2] ratios for USA manufacturing industries

	1954–68	1969–82
Total Manufacturing	1.16	0.99
Primary metals	1.29	0.97
Fabricated metals	1.29	1.42
Electronic machinery	0.92	0.77
Machinery (except electronic)	1.21	0.98
Motor vehicles	0.94	0.93
Other transportation	1.01	0.50
Stone clay	1.07	0.88
Food, beverage	1.14	0.94
Textiles	1.27	1.22
Paper	1.05	0.82
Chemicals	1.13	0.80
Petroleum	1.15	1.30
Rubber	1.05	0.81

[1]Sum of the undistributed profits and capital consumption allowances in the previous year.
[2]New plant and equipment expenditures including replacement expenditures in the current year.

Sources: Survey of Current Business, Feb. 1985 issue for investment expenditures, and *National Income and Product Accounts* for internal funds.

Table 1.2 *Internal funds/investment ratios for non-financial corporations in 11 OECD countries (averages of 1976–80)*

Country	IF/I (%)
United States	89.5
United Kingdom	88.0
Germany	80.1
Canada	76.5
Netherlands	73.9
Finland	68.4
Norway	65.9
Japan	62.6
France	61.6
Denmark	57.5
Italy	56.9

Source: OECD *Financial Statistics Part 3*: Non-Financial Enterprises–Financial Statements, 1985.

firms' survival, were treated as closely interrelated rather than as separate.

The first explanation that may come to mind for the failure of economic theory to set up a relationship between pricing, financing and investment decisions is the methodological approach employed by economic theory: the level of formalism reached in economic theory in terms of mathematical techniques does not lend itself to an analysis of such a complex interactive process. Methodological considerations are secondary, however, to the failure of neoclassical economic theory to set up a relationship between pricing, financing and investment decisions. This links, in turn, to the way neoclassicism portrays competition in terms of market structure. The conception of competition as a market structure focuses on exchange relations and on price behaviour to the exclusion of such important facets of firm behaviour as production, investment and finance. This has permitted the separate analysis of firms' pricing, investment and financing decisions without questioning the interaction that may exist between them. While this might have simplified the formalization of the theoretical considerations in the respective fields, it has not been without costs.

One cannot logically evade the interaction between firms' pricing, investment and financing decisions without eliminating the existence of fixed capital, that is to say by assuming that firms exist in only one period. If firms exist in only one period, there is no need for investment or financing because all the capital is consumed in that period. With fixed capital, firms' investment decisions have to be taken into account because the costs of production, or the competitiveness of fixed capital, in the following periods depend on current investment decisions. The continuous need to undertake investment in the multi-period horizon further implies a need to raise the funds to be invested, which in turn requires decisions as to the source of those funds (internal or external).

In conventional theory, firms maximize their short-run profits, given the restrictive assumption that firms know their demand curve without explaining at all how they acquired that knowledge. When conventional theorists try to introduce dynamics, the problem of the multi-period horizon and the uncertainty that arises from it are solved by changing the objective function from the maximization of profits to the maximization of discounted profit and/or expected profits. That is, time is introduced in the Newtonian sense without addressing the issue of fixed capital.[2] Investment behaviour does not enter into consideration because it is assumed that technology is exogenous and competition is in price only.

This particular conception of competition has been so pervasive in the history of economic thought that even diverse critics of orthodox theory, such as Marx and Keynes, have relied upon it. This is exemplified in the uniform profit-rate assumption in Marxian theory and the neoclassical synthesis of Keynes. Kalecki's 'degree of monopoly' theory is also not an alternative but a variant within the neoclassical pricing theory.[3] Baran and Sweezy have done the job of extending the same conception into the neo-Marxist framework.[4] Post-Keynesians have not been an exception to this general trend. As

Sawyer (1990) mentions:

> many of the post-Keynesian approaches have been rather static in the sense of taking the industrial structure (whether in terms of the degree of industrial concentration or in terms of an established price leader) as given, paying little regard to the process of change and the pressures of competition.[5]

What is lacking in post-Keynesian and other alternative approaches is that they fail to take account of the dynamics of capitalist economies, being shaped instead by the focus of existing theories.[6] For example, the focus of neoclassical price theory is the market structure. Market structure has also become the focus of post-Keynesian pricing behaviour as in Kalecki, Cowling, Eichner and other authors. Eichner, Wood and some other post-Keynesians have recognized the importance of investment in their analyses. However, the focus of those analyses has remained market structure with its underlying conceptual framework rather than the investment process in capitalist economies. This study attempts to break away from the market structure focus of earlier studies by adjusting its focus towards the dynamics of capitalist economies through the conceptualization of competition as a survival process. By doing so, it suggests an alternative conceptual framework for the post-Keynesian approach.

THE NEED FOR AN ALTERNATIVE CONCEPT OF COMPETITION

The concentration on market structure and price competition has deprived economic theory of a key organizing concept, capable not only of relating the pricing, investment and financial-structure decisions of firms but also of explaining some basic features of the capitalist development process. There are two features of capitalist economies that have exerted themselves continuously over the last two hundred years, which economic theory has been unable to account for:

- *Rapid technological change*   The main body of economic

theory simply assumes that technology is an exogenous
parameter or treats it as an unexplained residual as in
Solow's famous article.[7] However, rapid changes in technology have been the most continuous and important
feature of capitalist economies that deserve to be the focus
of any theoretical approach that aims at analysing capitalist economies.

- *The uneven development of regions and nations and the
  shifts in centres of power and growth over time.*   For example, the British dominance in the early twentieth century
  has gradually declined and US economic superiority has
  characterized the greatest part of the post-World War II
  period to be increasingly shadowed by the success stories
  of Japan, Germany and newly industrialized countries
  (NICs) since the late 1960s. This has focused attention on
  the importance of institutional factors, such as the role of
  the state, cultural factors, financial institutions and so on,
  that may account for these changes. The institutional
  structure of the economy has not been studied by economists but by political and business strategists. The rapid
  economic development of Japan in the post-World War II
  period, for example, has brought Japanese industrial policies to the centre of public and academic discussions in the
  last decade. Discussions of industrial policies in other
  countries (especially in the USA and the UK) have
  increasingly led to the analysis of the relationships
  between the real and financial sectors of the economy[8] and
  the implications of different financial systems for the process of growth.

  The deficiency of a conception of competition that concentrates exclusively on market structure is that price behaviour
alone does not encompass the means by which firms try to
survive in a competitive environment nor their relation to the
institutional structure of the economy. Both rapid technological change and the uneven development of regions or nations
are primarily results of the survival process taking place in
certain institutional structures existing at a specific time-point
in history. The basic characteristic of the survival process in

capitalist economies is that firms are under continuous pressure to innovate to stay competitive. This raises the survival struggle beyond simple reproduction to reproduction at a continuously expanding level. The resulting technological dynamism is unique to the capitalist system. Since a particular form of the survival struggle develops in a particular institutional structure, the dynamics of capitalist economies show uneven development in the international context due to the historical specificity of the institutional structures in each country.

If we are going to capture the survival efforts of firms, their investment behaviour needs to be analysed together with their pricing decisions. The objective of this book is to provide a first attempt to conceptualize competition as a survival process, its operationalization and empirical testing.[9]

The conceptualization of competition as a survival process has several advantages over the conventional view of competition as a market structure:

- it is dynamic, as opposed to the static nature of the conventional conception, and technological change is explained rather than assumed;
- it provides a framework for the joint analysis of firms' pricing, financing and investment decisions; and
- the institutional structure of the economy becomes an integral part in the analysis of the competitive process because a particular form of the survival struggle develops in a particular institutional structure.

THE STRUCTURE OF THE BOOK

The structure of the book is as follows: Chapter 2 reviews the post-Keynesian literature on pricing and investment decisions. Both Kaleckian and post-Keynesian pricing models are considered to identify the weaknesses of these models and possible contributions that this study can make in this area. Chapter 3 reviews the conception of competition in economic theory so as to: emphasize the importance of the concept of competition in economic analysis, identify the inadequacies of that concept and lay the ground for a different conception of competition. The classical, neoclassical and rival concepts of competition are considered. Rival approaches include the Austrians, P.W.S. Andrews and workable competition. The contestability theory is also included to present the most recent position of neoclassical economists. A conception of competition as a survival process is developed (survival in this context refers to the firms' ability to make profits). Firms are established to make profits. However, the firms' desire to make profits brings them into collective interaction and competitive struggle. Firms which are able to make profits survive, while unprofitable ones disappear. The survival efforts of firms include all the economic activities of firms from pricing to production to investment and to financing which all enable firms to stay competitive and continue to make profits. A measure of competitive behaviour is suggested and the survival process concept is applied to explain the persistence of profit-rate differentials across industries.

The conception of competition of Chapter 3 is operationalized in the model presented in Chapter 4. The main theme of the model is that firms' pricing, profit and financing decisions are related to their investment decisions. These investment decisions determine the amount of profits firms set out to earn given the assumption about the financial system of the economy.

The basic hypotheses of the model, about the pricing and financing behaviour of firms, are tested econometrically in Chapter 5. Pricing behaviour can be described as profit targeting. Firms, on the basis of their costs and investment decisions, target their profits. Profit-targeting behaviour is tested at the two-digit Standard Industrial Classification (SIC) level for the US manufacturing industries. In the second section of Chapter 5, the differences in internal financing ratios across the manufacturing industries in the USA are econometrically tested.

Chapter 6 explores the institutional assumption of the model presented in Chapter 4 from comparative and international perspectives. The financial systems in Germany, Japan and the USA are analysed from the viewpoint of their implications for firm behaviour. The impact of financial systems on the technological dynamics of countries and on the financing patterns across countries is tested econometrically.

Chapter 7 is about the changing importance of national institutions in the dynamics of world economy. It specifically focuses on the internationalization of the financial markets and its implications for competitiveness in the world economy. The last chapter summarizes the conclusions of the book.

NOTES

1. Anderson (1964), Creamer, *et al.* (1960), Duesenberry (1958).
2. For discussion of Newtonian versus historical time see O'Driscoll and Rizzo (1985, Chapter 4).
3. See Cowling (1982).
4. Baran and Sweezy (1966).
5. Sawyer (1990, p. 58).
6. For post-Keynesian views on several subjects see Sawyer (ed.) (1988). Arestis and Kitromilides (1990) present recent contributions to post-Keynesian approach. Apart from these, Caldwell (1989) assesses the post-Keynesian methodology and Sawyer (1990) raises a range of issues concerning post-Keynesian approaches to industrial economics.
7. Solow (1957).
8. Hu (1975), Carrington and Edwards (1981), Zysman (1983).
9. For a reader who is suspicious of the wide acceptance of the conventional conceptual framework in the face of the lack of empirical evidence for the models it uses and its inability to even account for the most prominent features of capitalist economies, I refer two sources: Kuhn (1970) and Ward (1972, 1979). Kuhn explains in general the reasons why specific paradigms continue to dominate different fields of science even though they lack the explanatory power; Ward develops Kuhn's ideas in the context of economic theory.

2. A Critical Review of the Post-Keynesian Theory on Pricing and Investment Behaviour

This chapter examines the post-Keynesian theory on pricing and investment behaviour to identify the possible contributions that can be made in this area. Post-Keynesian theory builds a realistic framework over neoclassical theory in explaining firms' pricing and investment behaviour. It suffers, however, from conceptual weaknesses inherited from the neoclassical theory. This chapter suggests that a further development of the theory is possible if the pricing and investment decisions are considered in a framework that is based on a survival concept of competition rather than the market-structure conception of the neoclassicals.

Post-Keynesian models fall into two groups in terms of the objectives of firms and the determinants of the mark-ups they specify.[1] Models in the first group (Kaleckian models) are based on the work of Kalecki and are further developed by Cowling. This group retains the profit-maximization objective and explains the size of the mark-up by the degree of monopoly or by concentration ratios, as in the work of Cowling. The second group of models provides a link between the pricing and investment decisions of firms and emphasizes the growth-maximization objective. These types of models were developed by Eichner, Wood, Harcourt and Kenyon, Ong and Shapiro, among others. The link between pricing and investment is the essential feature that distinguishes the post-Keynesian theory from other approaches. For this reason, the models that link pricing and investment decisions are the main emphasis of this chapter. Kaleckian models are also reviewed, and models that provide a link between pricing and investment decisions are considered. The most developed representations of this strand of post-Keynesian theory are reviewed. The chapter also discusses some weaknesses of post-Keynesian theory which arise from reliance on the market-structure concept of competition and suggests the usage of a concept of competition as a survival process which is developed in the following chapters.

KALECKIAN MODELS

Under Kaleckian models, Kalecki (1971) and Cowling (1982) models are reviewed. The Kaleckian models base their analyses on the fact that advanced capitalist economies are characterized by the dominance of oligopolies. This view leads to the mark-up of price over costs to be determined by oligopolistic factors, that is, by the degree of monopoly.

Kalecki's Degree of Monopoly Theory

In his analysis, Kalecki made a distinction between goods whose prices are 'cost-determined' and 'demand-determined'. He considered the prices of finished goods as cost-determined, whereas the prices of raw materials were demand-determined. Post-Keynesians have followed Kalecki's distinction in their analysis of industrial goods based on the mark-up on some measure of costs.

In Kalecki's model, prices are a mark-up on unit prime costs:

$$p = mu + n\bar{p}$$

where

p = the price set by a firm for its product
$\bar{p}$ = the average of the prices of competing firms
u = unit prime costs which includes labour and material costs

m,n are constants reflecting the degree of monopoly of the firm

For the industry as a whole, prices are given by

$$\bar{p} = \frac{\bar{m}\bar{u}}{1 - \bar{n}}$$

where $\bar{m}$, $\bar{n}$ and $\bar{u}$ are averages for all firms weighted by output. Accordingly, 'the degree of monopoly' is equal to $\bar{m}/1 - \bar{n}$. As the degree of monopoly increases, the mark-up and prices will increase. Prime costs are assumed to be constant over the relevant range of output. So in the short-run the output level is determined by the level of demand, and changes in demand do not affect prices. This aspect of Kalecki's model is the common feature of all post-Keynesian models. In the short-run only changes in the degree of monopoly can affect prices. As regards the determinants of the degree of monopoly, Kalecki suggested the influence of trade unions, changes in the level of overheads in relation to prime costs, advertising and the degree of industrial concentration. He did not, however, develop his theory further than his suggestions leading to several criticisms. For example, Fine and Murfin (1984) note that 'the degree of monopoly stood more as a tautologous derivation of the mark-up of prices over costs rather than as an explanation of that mark-up'.[2] However, Sawyer (1985) argues that confusion on the theory of degree of monopoly results from the different usages of the term. When it is used to mean price-cost margin itself, it becomes a tautology. But Sawyer (1985) contends that Kalecki understood the degree of monopoly as the factors, such as industrial concentration, determining the mark-up.[3] Further development of Kalecki's model along these lines was done by Cowling (1982).

Cowling's Model

Cowling (1982) formally developed the relationship between mark-up and the degree of monopoly. In his model, the firm maximizes profits by taking into account the reaction of other firms in the industry to its output decisions:

$$\pi_i = p\, Q_i - C\,(Q_i) - F_i$$

where

π_i = profits for firm i
p = industry price
Q_i = firm i's output. Q = industry output
$C(Q_i)$ = variable costs for firm i
F_i = fixed costs for firm i

When firms maximize the above profit function, taking into account other firms' responses to its output changes, the precise relationship between the mark-up and the degree of monopoly is found (for derivation, see Cowling 1982). The determinants of the degree of monopoly are formally stated as:

$$\text{degree of monopoly} = \frac{a}{-n} + \frac{(1-a)H}{-n}$$

where

n = price elasticity of demand
$H = \dfrac{\Sigma Q_i^2}{Q_2}$ Herfindahl index of concentration
$a = a_{ij} = \dfrac{dQ_j}{dQ_i}\dfrac{Q_i}{Q_j}$

a measures the expected reaction by firm j to output changes by firm i. It is assumed to be the same for all firms.

There are three determinants of the price-cost margin: the level of concentration measured by the Herfindahl index; other firms' reactions given by a; and the industry price elasticity of demand. The higher the Herfindahl index, the degree of collusion, and the smaller the absolute value of the industry price-elasticity of demand, the higher will be the degree of monopoly, hence the price-cost margin. According to Cowling, the reaction coefficient takes values between zero and one. If we consider two extreme cases, when $a = 0$, which is the

Cournot assumption, then the degree of monopoly is equal to $H/-n$. If a takes the value of one, the perfect collusion case, the degree of monopoly becomes $1/-n$, which is the pure monopoly case in the neoclassical model.

Kaleckian models emphasize the degree of monopoly in contrast to the perfect competition bias of the neoclassicals. When the degree of monopoly is precisely defined, as in Cowling's analysis, Kaleckian models do not show any differences from the static imperfect competition models of the neoclassicals. Indeed, as in the Cowling' analysis, the Kaleckian model becomes a variant of neoclassical models.

POST-KEYNESIAN THEORY ON PRICING AND INVESTMENT BEHAVIOUR

The relationship between pricing and investment decisions has been a fundamental feature of the microeconomic foundations of the post-Keynesian analysis since the writings of Kalecki and Robinson (Kalecki 1971, Robinson 1971). It is the emphasis on this relationship that distinguishes the post-Keynesian models from other mark-up pricing models. The latter focus on factors other than investment, such as demand elasticity and entry barriers in neoclassical models (Bain 1956, Modigliani 1958, Sylos-Labini 1962, Gaskins 1971), the internal organization of the firm in the organization theory (Cyert and March 1963), and the industry structure argument of the administered price hypothesis (Means 1936). In post-Keynesian theory, movements in prices depend upon the requirements for internally generated investment funds and upon movements in normal production costs. The mark-up is related directly to the need to finance planned investment expenditures. Investments are influenced by the general state of business confidence and by the relation between the observed rate of capacity utilization and some desired rate.[4]

However, the emphasis on investment as being the independent variable is not a new theme introduced by post-Keynesians. Its origins go back to classical economists. In particular, Marx's emphasis on capital accumulation deserves an important place. Chapter XXV of Volume 1 of *Capital* mentions explicitly the relationship between profits and the financing of the accumulation by capitalists. It is clearly stressed that 'the rate of accumulation is the independent, not the dependent, variable'.[5] Unfortunately this point has not been integrated into the Marxian theory of competition. It was not until the 1930s that Keynes, Kalecki and Schumpeter emphasized the importance of the problems of investment and growth. Kalecki developed the relationship between investment and profits at the macro level but did not provide a basis for a micro-level analysis (Kalecki 1971). Schumpeter's concern with the investment and growth process was limited to a descriptive exposition (Schumpeter 1942).

The Schumpeterian analysis is developed more analytically by Richard Nelson and Sidney Winter who portray firm growth as an evolutionary process (Nelson and Winter 1982). They concentrate on the individual characteristics of firms, such as organizational capabilities and skills which theoretically determine firm behaviour. 'Routines' and 'search' characterize firm behaviour. Nelson and Winter provide a detailed analysis of technological change and the growth process but do not consider the relations between firms' pricing and investment decisions.

Post-Keynesians' distinctive contribution has been to provide a microfoundation that explicitly sets a link between pricing and investment decisions that is absent in the Keynesian analysis. Since the early 1970s, several such models have been developed. This theme is most fully explored by Eichner (1976) and Wood (1975). Other contributions include Harcourt and Kenyon (1976), Levine (1981), Ong (1981) and Shapiro (1981), among others. In the following section, Eichner and Wood's models are emphasized to bring out the essential features of the post-Keynesian models that provide a link between pricing and investment decisions. Eichner and Wood emphasize two different areas of the link that complement each other. While the 'megacorp' forms the centre of the analysis in Eichner, relationships between capital markets and firms gain importance in Wood. The weaknesses of Eichner and Wood that are pointed out in the final section also apply to other models. Shapiro's analysis is also reviewed as a representative of the extensions, suggesting the importance of technological considerations.

Eichner on Pricing and Investment Behaviour

In Eichner's model, firms maximize their long-run growth. With the firm presumed to have an extended time-horizon going beyond the current accounting period, the pricing decision can no longer be separated from investment planning. Because of their market power, large corporations are able to change their intertemporal reserve flows through price adjustments to obtain more internally generated funds. Any price adjustment alters intertemporal revenue flows in two ways:

- from the returns to the investment thereby being financed; and
- from the decline in sales over time caused by the higher price due to
    the substitution effect,
    the entry factor and
    government intervention.

Eichner obtains an implicit interest rate for internally generated funds by expressing, as a percentage, the ratio of the funds expected to be lost because of the higher price over the additional funds generated from the higher mark-up. Eichner replaces the conventional opportunity-cost concept used in evaluating the cost of internal funds (for example, see Dusenberry 1958). This provides the supply curve of additional investment funds, whereas the firms' demand curve for additional investment is simply the familiar *ex-ante* marginal efficiency of investment. The supply curve for additional investment funds is horizontal at the level of the market interest rate.

Figure 2.1 shows the relationship between the level of investment and the sources of finance. S_{if} is the supply curve of internally generated funds through the mark-up. The implicit

Figure 2.1

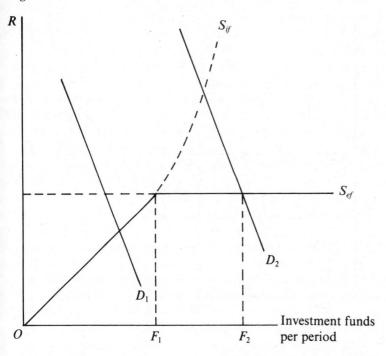

interest rate, R, increases as the amount of internally generated funds increases. Eichner assumes a perfectly elastic supply of external funds at a fixed interest rate, i, shown by the horizontal S_{ef} curve. The relevant portions of the supply curve of funds for the firm, then, is given by the heavy line OS_{ef}. The level of borrowing is determined by the level of investment demand represented by the D line. If the investment demand schedule is like D_1, all the funds will be supplied internally; if the marginal efficiency of the investment (MEI) schedule moves up to D_2, then OF_1 amount of funds will be supplied internally, and F_1F_2 will be financed externally.

Once the amount of borrowing is determined by the intersection of these two curves, firms set prices accordingly, taking into consideration the internal funds needed for investment purposes. Formally:

Figure 2.2

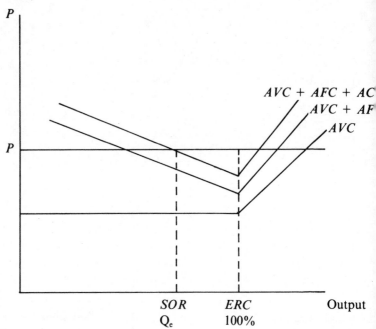

$$P = AVC + \frac{FC + CL}{SOR.ERC}$$

where

P = price set by the firm
AVC = average variable costs, assumed to be constant up to
    the level of capacity
FC = fixed costs
CL = corporate levy (the amount of funds generated from
    internal sources to finance investment expenditures)
SOR = Standard operating ratio (the expected operating
    ratio of the plant)
ERC = Engineer-rated capacity of the plant

The mark-up is determined by the fixed costs and the amount of funds needed from internal sources to finance investment expenditures. Figure 2.2 shows the costs curves that are relevant in Eichner's pricing model.

In Eichner's model the price is set by the leader in the industry and is adopted by other firms. In this way, there is a determinate solution in the model which sets an explicit relationship between firms' investment and financing decisions.[6]

Wood's Model

Wood's model is based on the effects of uncertainty and ignorance about the future of capital markets and company financial policy (Wood 1975). Rather than comparing the relative costs of different sources of capital, Wood simply argues that such a comparison is not made by firms. He points out the empirical evidence that industrial and commercial firms in Britain finance their investment largely through internal funds. He suggests that the assumed need for a comparison of the costs of funds is derived from unrealistic neoclassical assumptions about the functioning of capital markets.

The first of these neoclassical assumptions is that firms maximize their present value of net earnings. If firms maximize the growth rate of their sales, as Wood assumes, rather than the present value of their earnings it becomes likely that there will be investment projects which the firms would be keen to finance out of retained profits. This is because these investment projects may have a negative net present value when discounted at the interest rate that the firms could obtain if they were to make a loan at a comparable degree of uncertainty.

The second set of neoclassical assumptions concerns the functioning of capital markets:

- firms are indifferent between financing investment with internal funds and external funds;
- expectations of the future, while uncertain, must be objective, in the sense of being common to all agents in the capital market; and
- lenders must be willing to provide financing for any investment project provided that the rate of interest on the loan is sufficient to compensate them for what they regard as

the degree of uncertainty involved.

In the neoclassical analysis, the availability of finance is not a problem for firms. Firms are willing and able to finance, by borrowing, any investment project that they would otherwise be prepared to finance out of retained earnings. If this were true, however, there would be no need whatsoever for the firm to rely on retained profits.

Noting that these assumptions are unrealistic, Wood argues that:

- Firms will have different opinions regarding the profitability of investments than the financial markets. That is, expectations are subjective. In consequence, borrowers and lenders are unlikely to agree on what rate of interest is appropriate to any given investment project. Potential lenders may insist on an interest rate so high above that which the firm regards as appropriate to the degree of risk involved as to make it an unattractive proposition to undertake the project with borrowed money.
- The possibility of outright refusals to lend at any interest rate may leave firms unable to undertake investments which they deem necessary for their competitiveness.
- Borrowing money has certain risks which may not arise when investment projects are undertaken out of retained profits, such as the possibilities of bankruptcy and loss of control over the firm.

Wood sets out his model by claiming that firms strive to maximize their rate of growth of sales revenue subject to the 'opportunity frontier', which is largely a demand constraint, and to the 'finance frontier', which takes the dominance of retained earnings in the financing of investment into account. The capital account of the firm is the starting-point for Wood. In the capital account of a firm, gross investment expenditures plus the changes in the holdings of financial assets of a firm must be equal to the sum of the retained earnings and the change in the long-term external finance. The capital account constraint algebraically is as follows:

$$I + fI \leq g\pi + \chi I$$

where

I = Investment expenditures
π = Profits
f = Financial assets ratio, as the ratio of holdings of financial assets of a firm to gross investment
g = Gross retention ratio
χ = External finance ratio

In Wood's model, the target gross retention ratio is considered to be exogenous. It is largely determined by the dividend policy given the level of profits. The target external finance ratio depends on the managerial expectations of future profits and attitudes towards the risks and disadvantages of borrowing, unlike Eichner's implicit interest-rate calculations. The target financial-assets ratio, f, is determined by the need to provide a liquidity cushion against unforeseen contingencies. It is assumed to be constant.

From the above inequality, the level of profits needed to finance a given level of investment can be found as:

$$\pi \geq \frac{1 + f - \chi}{g} I$$

In Wood's analysis, prices are set at a level that will keep profit margins as low as possible to increase sales but high enough to finance investments. While Wood provides a consistent model, the validity of his model depends crucially on the behavioural assumptions that he makes on the parameters of the model.

Extensions by Shapiro and Ong

Following Steindl (1976) and Levine (1981), Ong (1981) and Shapiro (1981) suggested the importance of product and process innovations, and the lifecycles of industries, in the pricing

Figure 2.3

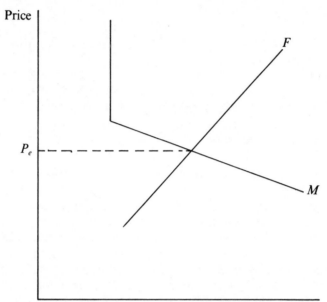

Potential Growth Rate/
Expected Growth Rate of Sales

and investment behaviour of firms.

Shapiro points out the importance of the product and process innovations after explaining the conflicting role played by prices in long-run growth maximization. Pricing has two different functions in the continuation of the firm's growth: higher prices imply higher profits to finance the firm's expansion; and prices will affect the market shares of the firms. So if the growth objective is going to be achieved, 'pricing has to be based on the principles of the maintenance and augmentation of (1) profit margins and (2) markets'. Following Steindl's arguments, Shapiro presents these points graphically.

In Figure 2.3 curve *F* represents the relationship between the firm's pricing policy and its potential growth rate, G_f. The potential growth rate will increase as the price increases because a greater quantity of internal funds will flow to the firm through higher prices. The curve M indicates the relationship between the firm's price and its expected growth of sales, G_m. The vertical segment is drawn on the assumption of an inelastic industry curve which implies that the firm's expected growth rate will be equal to the industry growth rate. On the elastic portion of the M curve, the firm can increase its sales by undercutting its rivals. The growth-maximizing price, P_e, is determined by the intersection of these two curves.

Shapiro recognizes the limitations of the analysis of price determination which was largely derived from Steindl. She introduces the notion of 'strategic price' that takes into account product and process innovations in the competitive process. This is also similar to Ong's (1981) 'growth-financing and product developing target prices'. Shapiro argues that it is the strategic price that is relevant for the firm's growth objective, not a pricing policy aimed at market dominance. If the firm charges 'a price less than the strategic one, it endangers both its current and future growth prospects. It spoils its market by accustoming its customers to a price lower than needed to realize its growth opportunities' (p. 99). However, the idea of strategic price, or the target price in the case of Ong, is not formalized and analysed in the context of a competition theory, leaving their contributions at a descriptive level.

In summary, starting with Eichner, post-Keynesians clearly recognize the importance of investments in attaining the long-run maximization of the growth objectives of firms. This sets the relationship between the corporate levy and pricing decisions. However, the process that makes investments so crucial in firm behaviour is not the focus of analysis, that is, the question what determines investment decisions is not answered beyond the marginal efficiency of the investment theory of Keynes. In Wood's analysis, the importance of the conditions and the possibility of non-availability of finance from capital markets is discussed. In a similar way to Eichner's, the analysis of the competitive process is left out in Wood's study. Consequently, the importance of the availability of capital is not integrated into an analysis of the competitive process. The importance of the competitive process is explained in the following section.

WEAKNESSES OF THE POST-KEYNESIAN THEORY ON PRICING AND INVESTMENT BEHAVIOUR

Post-Keynesians provide valuable analyses of firm behaviour incorporating long-run considerations and uncertainty. However, there seem to be two basic limitations that prevented the further development and application of these analyses which basically arise from the focus of the post-Keynesian models and the conceptual framework underlying that focus. These limitations are the lack of analysis of the investment process in advanced capitalist economies and the exclusive emphasis on the size of firms in post-Keynesian models.

The first limitation is that even though investment decisions play a critical role in post-Keynesian theory, post-Keynesians do not elaborate on the process by which investment decisions are made. Post-Keynesians, like neo-Keynesians,[7] appeal to the 'animal spirits' of capitalists in explaining the process by which investment decisions are made. As Geoffrey Harcourt notes, 'animal spirits certainly get a good run for their money in the post-Keynesian theory of investment'.[8] Peter Kenyon rightfully mentions that the concept of animal spirits is inoperative.[9] How can we explain the regularities of the capitalist development process, such as continuous investment and technological change, by the animal spirits of businessmen? If investment is central to the capitalist development process as post-Keynesians argue, its explanation should demand more than psychological factors. The systematic factors that lead to continuous investment and technological change in advanced capitalist economies should become the focus of the post-Keynesian approach.

The second limitation concerns the exclusive post-Keynesian emphasis on the internal structure of firms at the expense of the institutional structure of the economy. This is true for Eichner and Wood as well as for early post-Keynesians such as Kalecki and Robinson. The size of the firm is emphasized as the important institutional characteristic of modern capitalism, as Eichner's 'megacorp and oligopoly' and Kalecki's 'degree of monopoly' theories show. It is suggested that the institutional reality of capitalism is captured by the size of firms. This misplaced emphasis on the size of firms fails to recognize the endogenous nature of firm size in the capitalist development process.

The existence of large firms in an industry can be explained not by the lack of competition in the neoclassical sense, but by the technological dynamics of the industry. The possibility of economies of scale will naturally lead to the emergence of larger size firms. It is important to note that the industry structure (i.e. the number and size of firms in the industry) is an endogenous result of the competitive process. As the successful firms take over the market share of other firms, they become larger, and the number of firms may decline.

Meanwhile, the institutional structure of the economy is lost sight of, especially the relationship between industrial firms and banks. As Sawyer (1990) mentions, Eichner and Wood view 'the industrial sector as having largely freed itself of any control by the financial sector' (p. 65). For example, the basic fact to which Wood's model is addressed is that British firms finance their investment expenditures by internal funds. However, internal financing ratios vary from one country to another. While firms finance their investments mostly through internal funds in the securities-based financial systems of the United States and the United Kingdom, the internal financing ratio declines in the credit-based systems of Germany, Japan and France.

Both limitations originate from the conceptual framework employed by post-Keynesians. As in the Keynesian analysis, the neoclassical concept of competition as a market structure still prevails. As Sawyer (1990) argues 'an unsatisfactory feature of much of the post-Keynesian literature is that insufficient attention is paid to competition and rivalry'.[10] Post-Keynesians differ from neoclassicals in their exclusive emphasis on oligopolistic market structures. The weakness of neoclassical theory is not the emphasis on perfect competition, but the fundamental conception of competition, whether perfect or imperfect, as a market structure. The deficiency of the conception of competition that concentrates exclusively on market structure is that price behaviour alone does not encompass the means by which firms try to survive in a competitive environment nor their relation to the institutional structure of the economy. This also permits the separate analysis of firms' pricing, investment and financing decisions as in neoclassical theory without questioning the interaction that may exist between them. Attempts to do a joint analysis of pricing and investment behaviour based essentially on the neoclassical competition concept falls on *ad hoc* explanations for investment behaviour, as the animal-spirits approach of post-Keynesians shows.

An alternative conception of competition needs to focus on continuous technological change which has been the most important characteristic of advanced capitalist economies in the last two hundred years. Basing the conceptual framework on the survival efforts of firms provides the possibility for such a dynamic focus. The essential characteristic of the survival process is that firms are under continuous pressure to innovate to stay competitive. This raises the survival struggle beyond simple reproduction to reproduction at a continuously expanding level. Competition encompasses all the economic activities of a firm from finance to investment, to production, to exchange. Since these inter-related activities take place in different markets for labour, finance and products, competition is influenced by the interaction of different markets in the economy. This implies that an analysis of the competitive process requires an understanding of the whole institutional structure of the economy, especially the financial markets which determine the availability and conditions of funds to firms.

Donald Harris, for example, recognizes the importance of the institutional structure of the economy in the conclusion of his book on capital accumulation:

The profit-retention or pay-out policies of the firm and size of its mark-up or profit margin require theoretical treatment consistent with the position of the firm within the overall economic structure. For the individual firm, these relations govern its internal savings. Beyond this, the problem of savings for the firm becomes a matter of its access to finance, so that the structure and operation of the financial system have to be introduced. (Harris 1978: 288)

Fine and Murfin (1984) also point out that competition for

higher productivity is very much contingent upon access to the credit system.[11] In a similar fashion Fox (1987) argues that characteristics of the finance process need to be understood before knowing about the character of the firms entering the market.[12]

This study suggests a concept of competition as a survival process which handles the difficulties associated with the post-Keynesian models reviewed above. More importantly it operationalizes the concept of competition as a survival process and tests it econometrically. An important element missing in post-Keynesian models is that they lack empirical verification, for example, those of Eichner, Wood, Shapiro, Ong and others have not been tested empirically. This has been contradictory to the post-Keynesians' appeal to realism and also reduced the weight of their behavioural assumptions. For example, in his evaluation of Wood's model, Dougherty (1980) notes that virtually no empirical evidence is given with regard to the objective of growth maximization attributed to the management of a firm. By providing econometric support for the behavioural assumption of profit targeting proposed in this study, it is hoped that many more studies will be stimulated in that direction.

NOTES

1. For a similar classification of post-Keynesian pricing models, see Reynolds (1987, 1990) and Sawyer (1990).
2. Fine and Murfin (1984: 80).
3. Sawyer (1985: 28–36) presents other criticisms raised against the degree of monopoly theory and evaluates the validity of the criticisms.
4. For an introduction see Kenyon (1979).
5. Marx (1967: 620).
6. For a recent evaluation of the economics of Eichner, see Arestis (1989).
7. Neo-Keynesians are the Cambridge (England) -based or -inspired set of growth theorists such as Kaldor, and Pasinetti. The term post-Keynesians refer to those Keynesians, such as P. Davidson, A. Eichner, M. Kalecki, J. Kregel, H. Minsky, J. Robinson, G.L.S. Shackle, S. Weintraub and many others who work on microfoundations and stress the importance of uncertainty and finance in their work. However, under the broad definition of post-Keynesianism, neo-Keynesians should also be considered post-Keynesians as they

share same methodological concerns and have contributed so much along the same lines of research. Eichner (1979) and Sawyer (1988) provide samples of research that include the broad definition of post-Keynesianism.

8.   Harcourt (1980: 28).
9.   Kenyon (1980: 26).
10.   Sawyer (1990: 57).
11.   Fine and Murfin (1984: 140).
12.   Fox (1987: 33).

3. The Importance of the Concept of Competition

Since Adam Smith, competition has been the organizing principle for systematizing the fundamental forces at work in the capitalist economy and has provided the basis for the theories of value. The importance of competition is apparent in the core position given to the theory of perfect competition in economic analysis. For many, even for Schumpeter, who later had a different conception of competition, the model of perfect competition would always remain the 'Magna Carta' of the economic science, ensuring that its subject matter was a 'cosmos' not a chaos (Schumpeter 1934).

The influence of perfect competition has been so pervasive in economic analysis that almost every subfield of economic theory has been developed on that assumption. Even early sceptics such as Chamberlain (1933) and Robinson (1933) developed an alternative in reference to perfect competition. Their claim to add realism to the theory by 'imperfecting' it, thus has largely remained unsuccessful in providing an alternative. Not much later Schumpeter (1942) realized that the conception underlying any theory of competition, perfect or imperfect, needs to address the relevant aspects of economic change, especially the technological dynamics or 'creative destructiveness'.

The need for an alternative conception of competition is crucial for the development of a framework that considers the fundamental forces at work in capitalist economies, as these can not be dealt with in the conventional concept of competition. The concept of competition as a survival process may seem to be a familiar theme appearing in earlier writers such as

Marx and Schumpeter. However, these writers' valuable discussions on the survival process were reflected neither in the operationalization of their concepts of competition nor economic theorizing. This is most clearly exemplified in the equilibrium concept characterized by the equalization of profit rates in the Marxian theory, and the Schumpterian hypotheses on the relationship between the size of firms and innovative activity. It is the operationalization of the conception of competition as a survival process that distinguishes this study from earlier contributions. To give an example, there are no discussions in this book about equilibrium or about the size of the firms, as such discussions are not considered to be related to the survival struggle of firms. The continuous adjustment process, technological change, investment efforts, the institutional structure of an economy and relations between firms' pricing, investment and financing decisions are considered more important.

THE DEVELOPMENT OF THE CONCEPT OF COMPETITION IN ECONOMIC THEORY

Classical Economists

McNulty (1968) identifies two different forms of competition in the history of economic thought. The first one, which is associated with the classical economists, has been an 'ordering force'. This is somewhat analogous to the force of gravitation in physical sciences in assuring the allocative efficiency in the use of resources. The second form is a descriptive term characterizing a particular situation developed by neoclassical economists in the nineteenth century.

In classical economics, competition is an equilibrating force which adjusts the market price to its natural level by equalizing the rates of return on factors of production. This is due to the tendency of the factors to move from areas of low to high rates of return. In Adam Smith's theory, natural prices are composed of the normal rewards of the factors of production (wage, profit and rent). For Ricardo and Marx, the direct and indirect labour requirements are regarded, in the first approximation, as the centre of gravitation for actual prices (Semmler 1984a).

Although Adam Smith and other classical economists did not identify competition with a particular market structure as neoclassical economists do, they conceived it as taking place only in the market. This is clear in their exclusive emphasis on price competition. For example in Marx's theory, competition is a two-stage process:

● competition within sectors establishes market prices (and thereby unequal rates of profit within sectors due to the differences in efficiencies among the firms within sectors)
● competition between sectors establishes prices of production from those market prices on the basis of equalized rates of profit.

The equilibrium price vector is one which establishes the uniform rate of profit across the sectors through the mobility of capital from low-profit sectors to high-profit sectors.[1] Mobility of capital and the equalization of profit rates are results of a search for maximum profits by the capitalists. Dumenil and Levy (1987) place the mobility of capital as the central element in the classical analysis of competition.

While Dumenil and Levy argue that the model of the classical analysis is 'general' in the same sense as the general equilibrium of the neoclassical framework, Arrow and Hahn disagree with that view:

There is however, a very important sense in which none of the classical economists had a true general equilibrium theory: none gave an explicit role to demand conditions ... A general equilibrium theory is a theory about both the quantities and the prices of all commodities. The classical authors found, however, that prices appeared to be determined by a system of relations, derived from the equal rate of profit condition, into which quantities do not enter ... Thus, in a certain sense, the classical economists had no true theory of resource allocation, since the influence of prices on quantities was not studied and the reciprocal influence denied. (Arrow and Hahn 1971: 2)

The only movement that takes place in the classical competition theory is the one towards the equalization of the profit rates. It excludes investment due to self-expansion of capital which is central to the Marxian arguments. For example, Marx is explicit in conceiving competition as an ongoing struggle for survival. The principal weapon in this struggle, as Shaik (1978) also points out, is reductions in production costs. Reductions in costs enable capitalists to lower prices and drive their rivals out of the industry. In Marx's words 'the battle of competition is fought by the cheapening of commodities' (Marx 1967, Vol. 1: 626). Given the classical and Marxian emphasis on capital accumulation (Walsh and Gram 1980) and the continuous change in the structure of production,[2] the exclusion of investment behaviour from competition is a curious development in classical theory.[3] Auerbach (1988) argues that:

> The failure of the classical tradition to develop fully an analysis of the process of competition is related to its embracing of utilitarian psychology: a system which assumes that equalization 'perfectly' takes place is felicitously associated with the 'perfectly' rational entrepreneur, so that questions related to behaviour and to the process of equalization (or limitations to its consummation) may be subsumed and ignored. (Auerbach 1988: 17)

It is not possible not to agree with Auerbach's conclusion that 'the classical system failed to develop a theory of the evolution of competition which was linked to changes in behaviour, despite the potentialities inherent in its structure' (Auerbach 1988: 17). Followers of classical economists, especially of Marx, have not developed further the ideas the founders wrote about so extensively.

The Neoclassical Approach

The 'perfection' of the concept of competition as a market structure by neoclassical economists found its first formulation in the work of Cournot, who tried to specify the effects of competition as rigorously as possible (Dennis 1977: 198–205). According to Cournot, the effects of competition reach their limit with perfect competition (McNulty 1968: 642). In neoclassical theory, perfect competition is an equilibrium situation in which price becomes a parameter from the standpoint of the individual firm. That is, classical economists' preoccupation with competition as being exclusively a market process became exclusively a market structure for neoclassical economists. As McNulty puts it:

the single activity which best characterized the meaning of competition in classical economics – price cutting by an individual firm to get rid of excess supplies – becomes the one activity impossible under perfect competition. And what for the classical economists was the single analytical function of the competitive process – the determination of the market price – becomes, with perfect competition, the one thing unexplained and unaccounted for. (McNulty 1968: 649)

The conditions required for perfect competition cannot permit any other result to come out of the neoclassical analysis. These conditions may be stated as:

- a large number of buyers and sellers such that none of the participants can influence the market price;
- perfect knowledge of the conditions of supply and demand on the part of all the participants;
- no barriers to entry and exit, and perfect mobility of factors of production;
- a homogeneous product; and
- participants in the market act independently in their maximizing behaviour.

The conception of competition as a market structure took its current form in the late nineteenth century in Jevons and Edgeworth with later refinements by J.B. Clark and Frank Knight (Stigler 1957, McNulty 1968). Dennis, in his thesis on 'Competition in the History of Economic Thought', summarizes the developments in the conception of competition since then in the following words:

As classical 'free competition' was being transformed into neoclassical 'perfect competition', the scientific account of economic behaviour rendered by theorists grew more and more distorted, the almost absurd features of this 'perfect' type of behaviour being designed not to explain reality but to accommodate the special requirements of the new mathematical methods of analysis. While it is undoubtedly true that the arcane and increasingly rarefied concept of competition made possible the introduction and eventual refinement of mathematical logic in the economic calculus, a vital stage in the evolution of economic science, ironically the more persistent conse- quence of this turn of events has been that the scientific explanation of economic behaviour (as distinct from the pure logic of economics: rational choice and evaluation) drifted off down a blind alley, and at this point in the twentieth century has reached something of a dead-end. (Dennis 1977: iv–v)[4]

That is, the conception of competition as a market phenome- non has been developed only technically in the last hundred years and so has become narrower and more rigid to suit the needs of technical refinement. These developments have taken place even though the last hundred years have witnessed the most dramatic social, economic and technological changes in human history.

The influence of perfect competition has been so pervasive in economic analysis that almost every subfield of economic theory has been developed on that assumption. Critics, ortho- dox or radical, have suffered from a lack of questioning the underlying conception. They have attacked the assumptions of perfect competition such as the number and size of firms. By changing only the assumptions, they have continued to define monopoly and oligopoly in terms of their deviation from, and in reference to, perfect competition. This is as true for the orthodox attacks of Chamberlain (1933) and Robin- son (1933) in the 1930s as the radical attacks of Baran and Sweezy in the 1960s. The critics' net impact has been in the direction of strengthening the core position of perfect compe- tition in economic theory. The indeterminacies of imperfect competition have only made a stronger case for the mathema- tically determinate perfect competition.

Rival Approaches

The group of rival approaches reviewed here with the excep- tion of the contestability analysis, which is an extension of neoclassical theory, views competition as a process rather than as a situation. The common weakness shared among these approaches is that they never presented a consistent theoretical alternative to the market structure of competition or, as in the Austrian tradition, competition is rarely discussed in the context of formal theory. The purpose of reviewing these approaches is to show that there have always been economists opposing the static conception of competition. Even though these approaches failed to provide a consistent theoretical framework, they touched upon crucial aspects of dynamics that are also reflected in the conception of competition developed in this book. The contestability analysis's objective, however, has been different than these approaches, aiming to generalize the perfect competition of neoclassicals.

The Austrian approach

The Austrian approach has been one of the most vocal critics of the static conception of competition of neoclassical economists. This approach, represented by Carl Menger, Ludwig von Mises, Joseph Schumpeter and Friedrick Hayek among others, has extended to all areas of economics. Even though there are many differences in their views, this group of economists shares several common elements: methodological individualism; an emphasis on the incompleteness of knowledge and information, and on complexity and processes; and distrust of governments and complete trust in free markets.

The approach emphasizes the market process rather than market structures: 'Competition is by its nature a dynamic process whose essential characteristics are assumed away by the assumptions underlying static analysis' (Hayek 1948: 94). The most important neoclassical assumption that Austrians do not agree on is the assumption of perfect knowledge. In this respect, the importance of viewing competition as a process is clearly explained by Hayek:

If we consider the market for some kind of finished consumption goods and start with the position of its producers or sellers, we shall find, first, that they are assumed to know the lowest cost at which the commodity can be produced. Yet this knowledge which is assumed to be given to begin with is one of the main points where it is only through the process of competition that the facts will be discovered. This appears to me one of the most important of the points where the starting-point of the theory of competitive equilibrium assumes away the main task which only the process of competition can solve. The position is somewhat similar with respect to the second point on which the producers are assumed to be fully informed: the wishes and desires of the consumers, including the kinds of goods and services which they demand and the prices they are willing to pay. These cannot properly be regarded as given facts but ought rather to be regarded as problems to be solved by the process of competition. (Hayek 1948: 95–6)

The Austrian school places a great importance on entrepreneurs in the competitive process. Market opportunities are continuously exploited by entrepreneurs in their struggle for higher profits. However, the consequences of the actions taken by entrepreneurs are evaluated differently by the members of the Austrian tradition. For Kirzner (1973), entrepreneurs capitalize on market opportunities for higher profits and, thus, move the economy towards equilibrium in this process. For Schumpeter (1942), entrepreneurs' actions lead to 'creative destruction', that is to technological dynamics:

The function of entrepreneurs is to reform or revolutionize the pattern of production by exploiting an invention or, more generally, an untried technological possibility for producing a new commodity or producing an old one in a new way, by opening up a new source of supply of materials or a new outlet for products, by reorganizing an industry and so on. (Schumpeter 1942: 132)

The Austrian school presents a different attitude towards monopoly than that of neoclassicals. Competition is an ever-present threat for the businessman even if he is alone in his field (Schumpeter 1942: 85). The dynamics of the system are based on the profit motive. High or 'supernormal' profits encourage the rapid technological change observed in capitalist economies and should not be disrupted by government intervention. This is in sharp contrast to the neoclassicals, who view high profits as an indication of monopoly power and exploitation of the consumer.

Despite their valuable insights on ignorance and the market processes that contribute to the understanding of the dynamics of competition, the Austrians have not formalized their views. Indeed, they are opposed to using formal models and quantitative analysis to test their hypotheses, arguing that the uniqueness and ever-changing nature of economic processes do not permit measurable regularities in economic behaviour.

They have preferred literary modes of analysis which have limited their influence on the development of economic theory. Nevertheless, lately there has been a revival in interest in the Austrian approach especially in the public-policy area.

The Marshallian synthesis of P.W.S. Andrews

The conception of competition as a process was also taken by P.W.S. Andrews in his synthesis of Marshall's 'free competition'. Marshall's evolutionary views on the survival struggle of firms, as Reid (1987) mentions, were important in Andrews's analysis of industry. For Andrews, competition is a cost-reducing activity which takes place over historical time:

The realistic form that competition takes is a continual probing of the market by firms, increasing output of the product which looks more profitable, modifying design, shifting emphasis in response to the action of competitors and to pressures from customers, which again reflect actions or non-actions of competitors. (Andrews and Brunner 1975: 43)

As growing firms reduce their price, they will be able to expand their market share and secure their long-run survival. Unsuccessful firms face declining market shares, thus higher unit costs over lower output.

Andrews, arguing that 'a realistic theory of the firms needs to be integrated with a concept of the industry', provided a definition of an industry in terms of common techniques and processes. Accordingly, firms operate within an industry consisting of all other firms which use similar processes and possessing sufficiently similar backgrounds of experience and knowledge. That is to say, 'manufacturing substitution of product' is the basis of the industry definition. An industry includes firms producing different kinds of products. The market is a narrower concept, based on 'consumer substitution'. Since an industry may include many markets, firms' price-setting behaviour is constrained not only by its immediate competitors within the market but also by its competitors in other markets within the same industry.

Andrews' theory of competitive oligopoly is based on important facts which Andrews himself had observed first-hand through his industry investigations:

- In the short-run, the firm's average costs decline as its scale of production increases. In the long-run, competition puts pressure on firms to reduce their costs of production.
- Firms set prices as a gross profit mark-up over average direct costs determined by a normal flow rate of output chosen by the firm.
- The price is set by the price-leader taking into account entry threats.

Andrews' observations, however, have not led him to a complete theory of competition and pricing where the determinants of mark-up are explained and the role of the competitive process is integrated into firms' pricing decisions. This may be the reason why Andrews has not received the recognition that Lee *et al.* (1986) argue he deserves.

Workable competition

'Workable competition' was initiated by J.M. Clark in 1940 to develop an alternative to perfect competition for public-policy purposes. Markham (1950) states that 'economists recognizing the shortcomings of the theory of perfect competition in framing public policy for oligopolistic markets, recently have endeavored to define a more realistic standard of economic performance – workable or effective competition' (p. 349). However, 'since the concept owes its creation to a public policy need and not to the logic of abstract theory' (p. 349), its influence has been in terms of policy rather than the theoretical constructs it failed to develop.

As Markham points out, definitions of workable competition have been patterned largely after perfect competition. As a result, 'one of the obvious shortcomings of these definitions of workable competition which set forth a necessary set of conditions is that they neglect the dynamic forces that shape an industry's development' (1950: 360). This is clear in the development of Clark's ideas from a static conception of competition by amending perfect competition (Clark 1940), to explore dynamic criteria of competition (Clark 1955, 1961). For example, when stating the dynamic criteria of appraisal, Clark mentions that 'first comes progress in economical methods of production. Under competition, this implies that some take the lead and others follow, while managements are changed or firms are eliminated if they fall too far behind' (1955: 453).

There are certain insights in Clark's treatment which were never developed in a coherent theoretical framework but are crucial in the analysis of competition as a survival process as developed in this book. Clark states that:

the dynamic system is not one of elimination of profits, but one of erosion and re-creation, both of which are jointly essential. For the economy as whole, this process implies the creation, reduction and re-creation of differential rewards in different industries, as well as for different firms' (1955: 454).

However, Clark does not provide an explanation for why profit rates will be different in different industries.

Auerbach points out very important aspects of workable competition:

An examination of those workable competition criteria which depart from mainstream analysis reveal them to be of two kinds: first, they include structural variables which are not subject to easy quantitative treatment (e.g. the technological opportunities open to an industry) and secondly, there are a set of behavioural characteristics (e.g. the tendency of the firms in an industry to exploit these technological opportunities). (Auerbach 1988: 21)

These two aspects, the technological opportunities open to an industry and the tendency of the firms in an industry to exploit these opportunities, are very important in analysing the intensity of industrial competition in the historical context. Reducing the intensity of competition in an industry to market structure (e.g. number of firms), as neoclassical sympathizers of workable competition have done successfully, has considerably reduced the impact of workable competition in economic theory. A large part of the blame, however, falls on proponents of the concept, who failed to provide a consistent theoretical framework.

Contestability theory
While Clark moved from the static conception of competition

to a dynamic one in the development of workable competition, the static aspects have recently been developed rigorously by Baumol *et al.* (1982) in their contestability theory. The theory extends the results of perfect competition to all markets with any number of firms. A perfectly contestable market is defined as one in which the industry equilibrium is sustainable, in the sense that it offers no opportunity for profitable entry given the incumbent firms' prices. There are three main requirements of the contestability analysis:

- Potential entrants must be symmetrically placed with incumbent firms. That is, potential entrants should possess the same technology and sell to the same customers as incumbent firms.
- Exit is costless. Contestability theory assumes that there are no sunk costs. Once firms enter the industry, they can leave without incurring any costs.
- Price sustainability. Sustainability implies that incumbent firms do not change their prices in the face of entry or to prevent entry. Potential entrants assume that incumbent firms will not change their prices in the face of entry, thus base their expected profit calculations on the prevailing price in the industry.

Under these conditions of free entry and exit suggested by the contestability analysis, each firm will earn zero profits and set the price equal to marginal cost. If there is any positive profit in the industry, even for a short-time period, instantaneous 'hit and run' entry will eliminate the positive profit opportunities. These results hold true irrespective of the market structure and scale economies.

The restrictive requirements of the contestability analysis have been attacked both by neoclassical and post-Keynesian economists. For example, Schwartz and Reynolds (1983) argue that the requirements of the contestability theory are implausible: it is assumed that entry is instantaneous and at any scale. This is what Reid (1987) calls 'ultra-free entry' in which a new entrant can supply all of the markets at a price which slightly undercuts the one set by the incumbent firms.

Also, the assumption that the entrant can undercut the incumbent's price, make a quick profit and exit without a loss of fixed costs implies that the price response of incumbents is slower than the entry–exit process of the entrant. More importantly, it has been shown that the very small departures from the perfect contestability conditions invalidate the results of the contestability theory. For example, the existence of even small sunk costs eliminates the effects of contestable entry (Shepherd 1984).

Davies and Lee evaluate these neoclassical critics in a broader perspective in their post-Keynesian critique of the contestability theory. They argue that the criticism of the implausibility of the assumptions of the contestability theory:

is simply a criticism of the Friedman research methodology which underlies virtually all neoclassical theory. Consequently, we find the orthodox neoclassical assessment of the contribution of contestability theory to the neoclassical paradigm hypocritical: one can not single out the contestability concept for attack without simultaneously exposing to similar criticism the much more restrictive perfect competition and the other sacred principles of neoclassical theory (1988: 10).

They also point out that 'the perfectly contestable market really implies that all firms are in all markets, or, expressed alternatively, that there is only one market – the putty market – in which all firms belong' (p.18).

CRITICS OF THE CONCEPT OF COMPETITION

The inadequacy of the neoclassical conception of competition arises not so much from its rigidity but from its inherent weaknesses that have persisted since Adam Smith. The inadequacy of the conception of competition as a market structure has recently been recognized by several authors. Critics have emphasized the limitation of the concept to static analysis and exchange relations. Downie (1958), for example, concentrates on the efficiency differences between firms and growth, whereas Clifton (1977) focuses on the assumption of perfect capital mobility. Dennis (1970) and McNulty (1968) give critical accounts of the historical development of the conception of competition. While McNulty points out the absence of production and technological change, Byran (1985) focuses on the inadequacy of the institutionalist approach as it does not break away from the market conception of competition.

According to the critics, the conception of competition in conventional theory is static because it is not related to economic change and growth in a systematic way. Identification of competition as a market structure has diverted the concept of competition from analysing economic growth to analysing resource allocation. First of all, competition is conceived as a situation, a form of market structure, rather than a process. Secondly, the conception of competition as a market structure has concentrated solely on the market institution, thus on exchange relations rather than production relations. Since competition has been conceived as a form of institution rather than a pattern of behaviour, it is more useful to talk in terms of forms of competition rather than intensity of competition.

The form of competition in this context is determined by the number of firms that exist on the market. If the number of firms is infinitely large then it is called 'perfect competition', and if the number of firms in the market is less than infinitely large the competition becomes 'imperfect'. Alternatively, it is possible to define the form of competition by looking at the elasticity of the demand curves that firms are facing. That is, perfectly and imperfectly competitive firms differ only with respect to the elasticity of the demand curves they face. The analytical function of competition has been to get prices down to the level of marginal costs. The determinants of cost have not been explained. Yet, the cost of production is central to the process of competition. Costs of production differ across firms in an industry at any point in time and also through time.

The effect of assuming the cost of production as given amounts to assuming away the most crucial elements of competition, investment and technological change. Firms that produce at lower costs than their rivals compete out their rivals. In order not to be competed out, firms continuously try to reduce the costs of production. The reductions bring about changes in technology and growth which are the most prominent characteristics of capitalist economies. In the absence of investment and technological change, what is left is exchange relations in a static framework. Stigler (1957) and McNulty (1968) explain this by noting that economists have confused 'the market institution' with competition.

One can synthesize the contribution of the critics by defining competition as an interactive process of exchange and production. However, the inter-relationship between the different dimensions of this process has yet to be analysed by the critics.[5] More importantly, the process itself is not defined. This is in contrast to the neoclassical approach, where competition is a 'situation' defined in terms of 'market' as a form of market structure. The importance of defining the situation in terms of market is that neoclassical economists have been successful in operationalizing their conception of competition, so successfully that they have been able to use it to construct a rigid analytical core. The extensive use and importance of demand curves is a good example.

The success of the neoclassical operationalization has even influenced people who believe that competition should be conceived as a 'process' rather than a situation. For example, Baran and Sweezy's 'monopoly capitalism' or Kalecki's 'degree of monopoly' approaches are examples of operationalizing the conception of competition as a process in terms of 'market'. These authors treat capitalist development in terms of certain phases – competitive and monopoly phases which are distinguished by the size of the firms that exist on the market. It is thought that historical periodization of the competitive process' into such stages differentiates these approaches from neoclassical precedents. The dynamic dimension of defining competition as a process is essentially lost in these approaches since the 'firm size' is a static structure unless its evolution is taken as the subject of analysis. It is not at all ironic that the Kalecki's 'degree of monopoly' is formalized no differently than neoclassical pricing theories (see Cowling 1982).

THE CONCEPTION OF COMPETITION AS A SURVIVAL PROCESS

Survival implies firms' ability to make profits; firms are established to make profits. However, this desire coerces the firms into the necessity of making profits in the collective interaction of firms. Firms which are able to make profits survive, whereas the unprofitable ones eventually disappear. Unless firms are able to turn their desire to make profits into the ability to make profits, their very existence becomes questionable. Competition is a process which results from firms' drive for accumulation but also exerts itself upon that accumulation process. As Marx puts it:

> Competition makes the immanent laws of capitalist production to be felt by each individual capitalist, as external coercive laws. It compels him to keep constantly extending his capital, in order to preserve it, but extend it he cannot, except by means of progressive accumulation. (Marx 1967: 592)

Alchian is very clear on the necessity of making profits:

> In an economic system the realization of profits is the criterion according to which successful and surviving firms are selected ... Realized positive profits, not maximum profits, are the mark of success and viability. It does not matter through what process of reasoning or motivation such success was achieved. The fact of its accomplishment is sufficient. This is the criterion by which the economic system selects survivors: those who realize positive profits are the survivors; those who suffer losses disappear. (Alchian 1950: 210)

Survival is a relative process as Alchian further explains that:

> The pertinent requirement – positive profits through relative efficiency – is weaker than 'maximized profits', with which, unfortunately, it has been confused. Positive profits accrue to those who are better than their actual competitors, even if the participants are ignorant, intelligent, skilful, etc. The crucial element is one's aggregate position relative to actual competitors, not some hypothetically perfect competitors. As in a race, the award goes to the relatively fastest, even if all the competitors loaf. Even in a world of stupid men there would still be profits. Also, the greater the uncertainties of the world, the greater is the possibility that profits would go to venturesome and lucky rather than to logical, careful, fact-gathering individuals. (Ibid.)

Brenner adds that 'the perception of falling behind one's "fellows", and the feasibility of jumping ahead, induces individuals to be more driven' (Brenner 1987: 30).

To sell their products, firms cannot exceed the prevailing market price for long. At the same time, their ability to make profits at the market price is determined by their costs of production. If their costs of production are higher than the market price they will be losing money rather than making money. Firms are, therefore, under continuous pressure to reduce their costs of production. The costs of production are determined by many factors, including management, technology and organization. Reductions in the costs of production may take different forms: new and/or better quality products, new management structures or new processes, in short by the development of new technologies.

The development of new technologies is embodied in firms' investment efforts. For this reason, firms' ability to survive depends on the success of their investment efforts. Firms which are successful in reducing their costs of production relative to other firms will eliminate the other firms' ability to make profits.

The continuous nature of the investment efforts by firms also reveals their attitude toward the uncertain future facing them. Uncertainty leads firms to take account of various possibilities, a matter of survival for firms. Firms do not know in advance which aspects of the technological dynamics are being explored by other firms. By undertaking investments, firms explore those aspects of the technological dynamics that they think are the most profitable and the possible ones to be searched by other firms. This reduces the possibility of lagging behind other firms and losing the competitive edge. As Klein notes:

If firms could make perfect predictions of their competitors' behaviour they would have no need to insure themselves against uncertainty by generating new ideas, and smooth progress could never occur! (Klein 1977: 23)

This is in contrast to the standard approach where uncertainty is dealt with by assigning subjective probability distributions into agents' decision-making about the unknown variables.

As Vickers puts it:

The assignment of probabilities to future possible outcomes, either in the form of assumedly objectively given probability distributions or subjectively assigned probability distributions, is actually machinery inapplicable to decisions under uncertainty, for knowledge is the antithesis of uncertainty; it is the abolition of uncertainty. Thus the assignment of a probability distribution to possible outcomes involves the assertion that if the same event were to be repeated a large number of times, a designatable outcome would actually emerge in a pre-specifiable proportion of the instances. This, it can be said, is an assumption of knowledge that disqualifies the probability calculus for the tasks we have in view, quite apart, as we have pointed out, from the disqualification that arises from the uniqueness of the preponderant number of economic decision situations. (Vickers, 1978: 140)

The uniqueness of economic decisions arises from the fact that they are taken at a point in history, and the historical time is irreversible and is not replicable. Decisions are taken on the basis of the structures and relationships existing at a certain point in time and specific to that time. Once decisions are taken and acted upon, the structures and relationships that form the basis of the next decisions are changed. It is no longer possible to go back and take decisions differently than already made. This is because structures and relationships, the environment, that guided the earlier decisions are no longer in existence. There is uncertainty about how the decisions taken will affect current structures and relationships. The knowledge of the interactions between decisions and structures that existed in the past are not helpful in predicting the interactions between decisions and structures that will prevail in the future. This is because past decisions and structures were specific to the time at which they occurred. This uncertainty leads firms continuously to undertake investments that will help the formation of structures and relationships that will favour themselves.

Firms' investment efforts can be seen as firms' efforts to exploit the industry's technological dynamics. Firms' success in this pursuit is subject to the historical circumstances, in two ways:

• The industries go through different stages. In the early and immature stage, the growth rate of industries are rapid and technological opportunities are vast. As industries mature, growth rates slow down and technological opportunities begin to decline. In different stages of industries, thus a different set of opportunities is available to firms.

• Firms' utilization of these opportunities is determined by the overall dynamics of the economy, including the institutional environment. Firms search for opportunities in response to their environment. Exploitation of certain opportunities by firms is subject to the limits set by the environment. For example, in the 1970s the growth of the mini steel plants was in response to increasing import competition in a declining industry as well as the exploitation of certain technological opportunities in response to the specific circumstances of the mid-1970s.

Thus, history does matter in the actual development of the competitive process.

Since different industries have different technological dynamics, it is only natural to expect that their development pattern and industry structure will be different. The existence of large firms in an industry can be explained not by the lack of competition in the neoclassical sense, but by the technological dynamics of the industry. The possibility of economies of scale will naturally lead to the emergence of larger size firms. It is important to note that the industry structure (i.e. the number and size of the firms in the industry) is an endogenous result of the competitive process. As successful firms take over the market share of other firms, they become larger, and the number of firms in the industry may decline. The meaning of an observed market structure depends on the historical path by which it was reached.[6] This is in contrast to the neoclassical conception of competition. In reality, it is the competitive process that determines the market structure.

The central role of investment in the competitive process is reflected in the inter-relationships among the economic activities of a firm. A firm's ability to set prices, and thus its profitability, depends on its production efficiency. In a dynamic context, production efficiency is determined by the efficiency of investments undertaken by the firm. In turn, it is the availability of profits and loans that enable the firm to undertake the investments that it deems crucial for its competitiveness. The availability of capital to new firms and the conditions of availability are determined by the financial system. This implies that the pricing, financing and investment decisions of firms are influenced by the financial system and should be taken into account when such decisions are made. A new entrant must convince the decision-makers in the financial system that the entry is a profitable investment for lenders or investors. Easiness of obtaining capital depends on the institutional characteristics of the financial system. These characteristics may vary from the nature of the relationships between incumbent firms and financial institutions to the degree of centralization of the financial system as explored in Chapter 6.

Competition encompasses all the economic activities of a firm from finance to investment, to production, to exchange. Since these inter-related activities take place in different markets for labour, finance and products, competition is influenced by the interaction of different markets in the economy. For this reason, an analysis of the competitive process requires the understanding of the whole institutional structure of the economy. As mentioned above, the nature of the interaction between firms and financial markets affects the availability of funds for investment. If incumbent firms are favoured at the expense of potential entrants in utilizing the financial markets, this may reduce investment pressure on firms with a dominant position without endangering their ability to make profits. This may sustain the dominance of the favoured firms in the economy and may weaken the relationships that exist between their investment, pricing and financing decisions. This may lead to a rent-seeking behaviour in the economy without inducing technological change.

The institutional structure that exists in most developing countries provides the best example for this type of competition. The close relationship between the banks and dominant firms, indeed the co-ownership of the banks and firms by the same family groups, effectively prevents the entry of potentially successful firms into the industry. This eliminates the pressure on the existing firms to innovate, which to a large extent explains technological stagnancy in the developing countries. In addition, when the access to loanable funds is limited to a small number of firms, thereby preventing entry into the industry, the rent nature of profits becomes more dominant because the profits made by the few firms can be attributed to the unique access these firms have to loanable funds. As financial markets develop and access to loanable funds widens, we see that existing firms feel an increasing pressure for innovation.

The financial system of an economy is important because it determines the intensity of domestic entry through the availability and conditions of capital. But one must also take into account the impact of foreign entry and/or imports on the competitive behaviour of firms. For example, there are differences in the competitive dynamics of countries with similar financial systems. The differences between less-developed countries and developed countries with similar financial systems, such as Japan and Germany, where there are close relationships between the banks and large firms, are a good example. Less-developed countries are characterized by technological stagnancy, whereas firms in Japan and Germany show technological dynamics. This example brings in the role of the state in the competitive process. Foreign entry and/or imports are decided by the policies of the state. Allowing foreign entry and/or imports, or their threat, may increase the competitive pressures on domestic firms. The state may also affect the competitive process by fiscal, monetary, industrial or antitrust policies. These policies may favour national firms over foreign firms, certain sectors over other sectors or even some firms over other firms within an industry.

Foreign entry forces firms to evaluate the costs of production and markets worldwide. Goods produced by foreign firms, taking advantage of, for example, relatively low foreign wages may endanger the survival of even the most efficient domestic firms. While the costs of production are being determined in the national context by the labour markets, financial system and state policies, product prices are determined on world markets. Under these conditions firms can no longer think in terms of domestic costs of production and markets and search for lowest costs of production and possible markets. The internationalization of production and the emergence of multinational firms just reflect the changing forms of the survival struggle in an historically dynamic environment. The historical changes in the environment that firms face are also affected by state policies as the developments in international economic policies in the last century and the recent policies towards integration of the European Economic Community show. For this reason, it is not possible to abstract the analysis of competition from the existing social and political structures.

To summarize, competition is a survival process in which firms' ability to make profits determines their survival. To survive, firms continuously undertake investments which bring about technological changes. Competition encompasses all of the activities of firms, including pricing, investment, and financing decisions. Institutional structures, ranging from the financial systems to the state, play an important role in the competitive process.

A CRITERION FOR COMPETITIVE BEHAVIOUR

The neoclassical competition theory provides several criteria to measure competitive behaviour. These include pricing, concentration ratio and profitability measures which reflect the market-structure conception of competition of the neoclassicals. According to the pricing criteria, if firms are price-takers perfect competition prevails. If prices are set by firms, depending on the number of firms, an oligopoly or monopoly exists. This way of evaluating competitive behaviour is a result of the 'quantity theory of competition' as Weeks (1981) puts it. The concentration ratio measures the market share of a certain number of firms. The number of firms usually ranges from four to eight. The four-firm concentration ratio measures the four largest firms' market share in the industry; if it is high relative to other industries' concentration ratios, it implies a lack of competition. Profitability measures vary from the rate of return estimates to calculations of profit margins. Again high profitability implies a lack of competition whereas zero profitability corresponds to perfect competition.

These measures are easily quantifiable, accounting for their wide usage. However, all of these criteria depend on the static conception of competition. Infering competitive behaviour from prices in a dynamic world where competition arises through technological changes does not say much about competition. Brenner (1987) notes that:

since people introduce new products and bet on numerous new competitive strategies either in marketing, the internal organization of the firm, or advertising practices, there are no standards to which one can just adapt. The answer is that pricing just becomes one particular strategy, a bet, an art. (Brenner 1987: 49)

Concentration ratios do not reflect competitive behaviour either. Concentration ratios may be high not because of lack of competition but because of the efficiency of firms in the industry and opportunities for economies of scale. In a similar way, the profitability of firms may be high in the industry because the technological dynamics of the industry may demand high profitability.

Brenner, who puts innovations at the centre of competition as in the survival concept of competition, suggests that:

no clear-cut behavior patterns can be derived by looking at the number of firms. Instead one must look at evidence on relative rates of innovations that indicates whether or not the decision makers take into account the risk of falling behind their perceived competitors. (Brenner 1987: 68)

He prefers an output-based measure such as the percentage of sales produced by new products in past years, arguing that:

the inputs into the creative effort were not measured in any meaningful way (indeed they can not be), it is not very surprising that the various indices built as indicators of this effort – expenditures on research and development (R&D), schooling of workers, number of employed scientists and engineers, having patent priority – failed to shed light on what *ex-post* turned out to be successful innovations. (Brenner 1987: 101)

Table 3.1 presents the percentage of sales produced by new

Table 3.1 *The percentage of sales produced by new products (products less than four years old)*

Industry	1960
Iron and steel	5
Nonferrous metals	8
Machinery	14
Electrical machinery	12
Motor vehicles	10
Fabricated metals	17
Chemicals	16
Pulp and paper	9
Rubber	2
Stone, clay and glass	9
Food and beverages	6
Textiles	9

Source: Brenner 1987. 107, Table 1.

products for US manufacturing industries in 1960. The range of the percentage of sales produced by new products changes from 2 per cent for the rubber industry to 17 per cent for fabricated metals. The chemicals, machinery and electrical machinery industries follow fabricated metals in new product introduction.

However, it is misleading to measure the competitive behaviour with an outcome indicator, for the very reason that Brenner mentions above. It is the intensity of competition between firms that needs to be measured. As Brenner states, the relationship between the efforts and results sometimes may not be close. This does not mean that firms are not putting forth their best efforts, or are not involved in an intense competition. But for some reason, these efforts do not produce marketable innovations. The reasons could be many.

- Firms may not have reached a technological threshold that would yield marketable innovations. Once that threshold is reached, new products might be coming out quickly. Reaching a technological threshold might be a long and costly process. Emphasizing only the output of that process would be misleading. In a similar fashion, when making comparisons across industries, if in some industries technological conditions permit the rapid realization of new products relative to other industries given the level of R&D expenditures, than an outcome indicator for competitive behaviour would be misleading.

● New products are only one aspect of technological dynamics. Improvements in quality and production processes of existing products are another. Taking into account only new products, then, would be an inadequate measure of innovative activity.

● It is difficult to define what constitutes a new product and then to measure the percentage of sales produced by new products. This is because the data on such a percentage are not published publicly, making such a measure less practical.

Technological change is the most important aspect and result of competition as a survival process. Firms are under continuous pressure to reduce their costs of production to survive. Reductions in the costs of production may take different forms: new and/or better quality products, new production processes, new management structures or new strategies in marketing; in short, by the development of new technologies in the broad sense of the word. A measure of competitive behaviour, then, should be related to the technological dynamics. The ratio of R&D expenditures (R&D) to investment expenditures (I) seems to be an appropriate measure of technological dynamics that reflects the intensity of competition. As competitive pressures on firms increase, they will try harder in bringing about new technological changes. R&D expenditures are the best indicator of competitive efforts. Since technological innovation is a risky investment, such expenditures measure the willingness of firms to commit themselves. The funds come out profits which also implies a relationship between pricing strategy and investment (as will be developed in the next chapter).

Taking the ratio of R&D/I expenditures rather than the level of R&D expenditures as the measure of competitive behaviour standardizes the measure for firm and industry sizes. The absolute level of R&D expenditures is not relevant because, depending on the size and technological nature of the industry, these expenditures may vary across industries without implying competitive pressures. The level of R&D/I ratio reflects competitive pressures more properly. Investment expenditures are undertaken to increase production capacity and also to improve technological capacity. In high- or low-growth industries, competitive pressures will be more correctly reflected in the ratio of R&D/I expenditures. Using I as the denominator, the life-cycle and cyclical factors are taken into account in measuring competitive behaviour; second, investment expenditures are used as the denominator rather than the conventional sales variable because the R&D/I ratio reflects dynamic competitive behaviour better than the R&D/sales ratio (see Chapter 5).

The ratio of R&D/I has several advantages: it is easy to measure and interpret, data on R&D/I are publicly available; it measures the competitive efforts of firms on a continuous basis contrary to the Brenners' measure of sales produced by new products; it is a measure free of the number of firms that exist in the industry, market structure loses its importance; it permits intra-industry, inter-industry and international comparisons of technological dynamics. The most competitive firms will be undertaking relatively higher R&D expenditures, whereas imitators will have low R&D/I ratios. High-technology industries will exhibit higher R&D/I ratios. In countries where competitive pressures are higher, industries will have relatively higher R&D/I ratios. International comparisons may also indicate the importance of the differences in institutional structures (see Chapter 6); and the interpretation of R&D/I ratios requires an historical and institutional evaluation of each case. For example, even though the market structure stays the same, import competition may increase the pressure on firms to innovate, depending on the nature of the industry, the extent of import competition and other factors. At the same time, import competition weakens the internal

Table 3.2   R&D/I ratios for US manufacturing industries (%)

Industry	1960	1957–79 average
Primary metals	9.9	9.54
Fabricated metals	24.2	18.30
Electrical machinery	83.0	76.52
Machinery	78.4	62.00
Motor vehicles	60.1	59.18
Stone and clay	11.3	13.01
Textiles	9.3	7.27
Food	7.7	7.47
Paper	7.3	9.46
Chemicals	61.6	53.32
Rubber	35.6	31.86

Source: National Science Foundation, *R&D in Industry*, several years; *Investments, Survey of Current Business*, February 1985.

sources of funds to undertake R&D activity.

Table 3.2 shows the R&D/I ratios for the US manufacturing industries for both 1960 and the 1957–79 average. The ratios for 1960 provide an opportunity to compare Brenner's measure with the one proposed in this study. The range of R&D/I ratios changes from 7.27 per cent for textiles to 76.52 per cent for electrical machinery.

EXPLAINING THE PERSISTENCE OF THE NON-UNIFORMITY OF PROFIT RATES

The uniformity of profit rates is central to the basic structure of both neoclassical and Marxian models. In both of these, equilibrium is characterized by the uniformity of profit rates across industries. The mechanism that provides that uniformity is the mobility of capital. As capital moves from low to high profit-rate industries, the supplies of goods in the former are reduced, whereas the supplies of goods in the latter are increased. The perfect mobility of capital thus assures the uniformity of profit rates across industries.

However, the real world is characterized by the persistence of non-uniform profit rates. Profit rates for 11 SIC two-digit manufacturing industries in the USA for the period 1957–81 are shown in Table 3.3.[7] Profit rates for industries are defined as the ratio of profits plus net interest payments to gross capital stock in each industry. As seen from Table 3.3, profit rates change widely from one industry to another. Since the table shows the profit rates at the SIC two-digit level, one would expect further divergencies as the data become more disaggregated. Dennis Mueller (1986) provided empirical evidence on the persistence of profit rates at the firm level. He tested the hypothesis that profits converge over time on a competitive level as suggested by the neoclassical and Marxian approaches, using time series data for 600 companies. He concluded that above- and below-average profits tend to converge back toward the mean of the sample but persistent differences in corporate profitability continue into the indefinite future. While Mueller's objective was to find out the importance of the industry and firm-specific factors to explain the persistence of differences in corporate profitability, the level of analysis appropriate for this study is industry. For this reason, the hypothesis of the equalization of profit rates is tested at the industry level.

Following the specification presented by Mueller, the equalization hypothesis suggested by the neoclassical and Marxian approaches is tested. In this specification, the intercepts from the regressions of profits on the reciprocal of time are compared.

$$\pi_{it} = \alpha_i + \beta_i/t + \epsilon_{it} \tag{3.1}$$

where

π_{it} = the ratio of deviations of the industry ith's profit rates from the average of all industry profit rates to the average of all industry profit rates

ϵ_{it} is assumed to be a normally distributed error term with zero expected value and constant variance

The intercept term, α_{it}, captures both the competitive rate and

Table 3.3 Profit rates in US manufacturing industries

Year	Primary metals	Fabricated metals	Electrical machinery	Non-electrical machinery	Motor vehicles	Stone	Textiles	Food	Paper	Chemicals	Rubber
1957	7.6	8.6	12.5	9.6	13.1	8.5	4.1	5.0	6.0	8.7	7.1
1958	5.1	6.5	11.1	6.4	4.0	8.4	2.9	5.8	5.3	7.4	8.0
1959	6.0	7.1	13.9	9.7	13.3	9.6	6.2	6.2	6.4	9.8	8.8
1960	5.3	5.5	9.1	7.5	12.8	7.5	5.4	6.2	5.7	8.9	6.9
1961	3.7	6.3	8.5	7.3	10.5	6.6	4.9	6.2	5.6	8.4	7.2
1962	3.9	7.4	10.3	9.4	16.4	6.6	6.1	6.3	5.5	8.4	7.6
1963	4.9	7.9	10.1	9.8	19.2	6.8	6.4	7.8	5.5	9.2	7.2
1964	6.1	8.5	8.9	12.1	19.8	7.8	7.7	7.6	5.9	9.9	7.6
1965	7.0	11.2	16.0	14.5	24.3	7.5	9.4	8.0	6.5	11.4	7.8
1966	7.1	12.3	16.4	14.0	19.8	6.0	8.5	8.3	6.8	10.8	8.3
1967	5.4	11.7	15.1	12.9	14.1	5.1	7.1	7.4	6.0	8.7	7.8
1968	4.1	9.3	11.8	10.8	16.5	5.5	8.1	7.4	5.7	8.5	8.2
1969	3.8	8.2	9.7	9.5	14.4	5.3	6.9	7.2	6.0	7.2	7.4
1970	2.8	5.5	6.4	8.5	8.1	4.0	5.9	7.6	4.7	6.3	4.5
1971	1.5	5.6	6.3	7.1	13.7	5.1	5.6	6.8	4.1	6.1	5.5
1972	3.3	7.0	8.5	8.7	14.9	5.7	5.4	6.3	5.1	6.8	6.2
1973	4.5	8.6	10.1	10.3	15.0	6.3	6.5	7.6	6.9	7.7	7.3
1974	7.0	8.8	7.2	9.9	6.7	4.6	5.2	7.7	6.8	6.9	5.9
1975	3.7	7.0	7.5	9.5	7.5	4.2	3.5	9.5	5.0	6.4	5.1
1976	3.5	8.0	6.9	9.0	12.2	6.0	6.1	8.1	5.8	6.9	5.0
1977	2.8	8.3	9.9	11.1	13.9	5.7	8.0	7.6	5.2	5.9	5.7
1978	4.1	8.5	10.8	10.1	12.3	5.7	5.7	7.4	5.2	5.4	5.9
1979	4.6	8.9	8.9	9.9	9.0	6.1	5.0	6.9	5.8	5.8	5.3
1980	2.9	6.8	8.5	9.1	3.2	4.1	4.4	6.6	4.5	4.4	3.3
1981	3.3	6.4	7.7	8.7	7.0	2.7	4.0	6.6	3.9	5.6	4.3

Figure 3.1

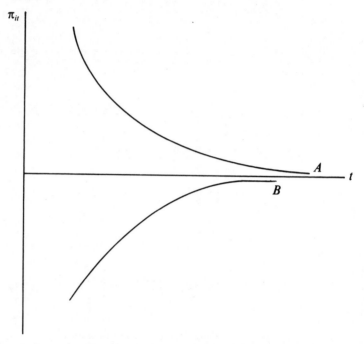

the permanent industry rents. If the equalization hypothesis of the neoclassical and Marxian worlds is valid, the estimated permanent industry rents should be zero for all industries, that is, the αs should be equal for all industries. Equation 3.1 is also useful for testing whether there is a tendency for profit rates to equalize. For this, the sign of β should be examined. Positive βs imply falling profit rates, while negative βs imply that they are rising.

Figure 3.1 gives the graphical explanation: if the industry i's profits are above the average profit rate at time $t = 0$, the equalization hypothesis implies that it will fall along a path like A to the average rate through time; less than average initial returns will follow a path along one similar to B to return to average rates.

Table 3.4 presents αs and βs for 11 two-digit US manufac-

Table 3.4   *Estimations of αs and βs for 11 US manufacturing industries (1957–79)*

Industry	α	β	Error process
Motor vehicles	0.771	−0.482	OLS
	(7.18)	(−1.18)	
Machinery	0.317	−0.345	OLS
	(9.38)	(−2.7)	
Electrical machinery	0.219	0.454	OLS
	(4.33)	(2.37)	
Fabricated metals	0.061	−0.118	AR2
	(1.24)	(−0.78)	
Food	0.02	−0.517	AR2
	(0.32)	(−2.43)	
Chemicals	−0.013	0.08	AR2
	(−0.31)	(0.64)	
Textiles	−0.153	−0.434	OLS
	(−5.14)	(−3.84)	
Rubber	−0.166	0.226	OLS
	(−5.40)	(1.94)	
Paper	−0.25	−0.04	AR2
	(−6.44)	(−0.36)	
Stone	−0.24	0.33	AR1
	(−4.78)	(2.07)	
Primary metals	−0.476	0.426	OLS
	(−12.5)	(2.95)	

Note: t-statistics are in parentheses. The error process indicates the method used in the presence of serial correlation.

turing industries estimated from equation 3.1 for the period 1957–79. In each industry, the profit rates are defined as the ratio of profits plus net interest payments to gross capital stock. As seen in Table 3.4, there are significant differences in the profitability across industries. αs for 8 out 11 industries are significantly different than zero; furthermore, the sign of βs show the persistence of the non-uniformity of profit rates rather than a tendency toward the equalization of profit rates.

Out of five industries with above-average profit rates, two have a significant negative ß sign indicating rising profit rates. Only the electrical machinery industry's profit rates tend to move to the average. Out of six industries with below-average profit rates, three have a significant positive ß sign, implying falling profit rates. These results show that the profit-rate differentials persist across industries. The question of why the neoclassical and Marxian theories build their equilibrium notion on the tendency of profit rates to equalize or on the uniformity of profit rates therefore needs serious consideration.

The uniformity of profit rates argument rests on the assumption of perfect capital mobility. This assumption confuses financial capital with fixed capital. As Clifton (1977) notes, Adam Smith's concept of competition was intended for a world of merchant capital rather than a world of fixed capital. Merchant capital is entirely free to move to sectors of high returns because it is not committed to production. The merchant can restore the liquidity of his capital by selling the commodities he holds, and invest in commodities with a higher expected return.

In a world of fixed capital, once financial capital is committed to production activity it becomes immobilized. At the end of the production period, partial liquidity comes from the sale of products produced by the fixed capital. A firm has the option of selling the fixed capital at a loss (if the rate of return is lower than the average) or preserving the competitiveness of its fixed capital by continuous investment in it. To give an example, let's assume that a firm invests its financial capital in an industry on the basis of expected returns (r_e) at the beginning of period 1. That is:

$$r_e = \frac{\pi_e}{P_k} \tag{3.2}$$

where

r_e = expected return
π_e = expected profits
P_k = price of fixed capital

It is assumed that, ignoring depreciation, the value of capital at the end of the period will be equal to its initial value. That is, there are no capital gains or losses. Now let's assume that there is a technological innovation in the industry. If a firm does not undertake investment to modify its fixed capital in this period, it will not be competitive in the following periods, so the assumed scrap value of the physical capital at the end of the first period will depend on the mobility of capital: if the fixed capital is mobile, then the firm can sell the physical capital at its initial value, P_k, and leave the industry; if the fixed capital is not mobile, then depending on the degree of mobility, the scrap value of the capital will approach zero. It will be zero when it is completely immobile. That is, capital mobility is defined by the ratio of recovery of the initial value, P_k, of the physical capital. If, for simplicity, it is assumed that actual profits earned, π_a, equal expected profits, π_e, then the actual rate of return (r_{al}) when investment is not undertaken is as follows:

$$r_{al} = \frac{\pi - \delta P_k}{P_k} \qquad (3.3)$$

where

r_{al} = the actual rate of return when investment is not undertaken

π = actual profits which are assumed to be equal to expected profits

δ = the coefficient of capital immobility

$0 \leq \delta \leq 1$

If $\delta = 0$, the fixed capital is perfectly mobile and the firm can recover the full value of its initial investment in fixed capital. If $\delta = 1$, the fixed capital is completely immobile and the firm cannot receive any value for its initial investment. This is because the technological change has completely eliminated the value of the initial investment.

When equation 3.3 is written as follows

$$r_{a1} = \frac{\pi}{P_k} - \delta$$

$$(3.4)$$

it can be easily observed that if $\delta \geq \frac{\pi}{P_k}$ than $r_{a1} \leq 0$.

That is, a very small amount of immobility may make the rate of return negative when the firm does not undertake investment to stay competitive in the industry in the face of technological change.

If investment is undertaken, the fixed capital will regain its value because it is assumed that its ability to bring cash flow in the following periods will be restored. If the investment is undertaken, then the actual rate of return (r_{a2}) for the firm is:

$$r_{a2} = \frac{\pi}{P_k + \Delta K}$$

$$(3.5)$$

where

r_{a2} = the actual rate of return when the investment is undertaken

ΔK = the amount of investment undertaken to keep the fixed capital competitive

If the firm undertakes the investment, it will have a lower rate of return but a positive one. Even though the profit rate is low, the firm may stay in the industry as long as the rate of return is at a level to keep the firm competitive in the industry. Formally, the firm will stay in the industry if and only if

$$r_{a2} \geq r_{a1}$$

$$(3.6)$$

That is,

$$\frac{\pi}{P_k + \delta K} \geq \frac{\pi}{P_k} - \delta$$

$$(3.7)$$

or,

$$\delta \geq r_e - r_{a2}$$

$$(3.8)$$

The conditions to stay in the industry can be checked from equation 3.8. If $r_{a2} = 0$, then $\delta \geq r_e$ which is the value that makes $r_{a1} \leq 0$ from equation 3.4. If the value of $r_{a2} \geq 0$, then equation 3.8 implies that even if the immobility of capital is very low, less than $\delta = r_e$ which makes $r_{a1} = 0$, firms stay in the industry. The firm stays in the industry as long as r_{a2} is positive, which is always true, as can be verified from equation 3.5, unless π is negative. It can be concluded that with technological change, profit rates are evaluated at the industry level taking into account the rate of technological change in the industry.

When technological change is introduced, the neoclassical and Marxian models, which assume capital mobility, are no longer valid because the capital mobility assumption essentially boils down to a no-technological-change assumption. This can be shown by examining the case where $r_e = r_{a2}$ in equation 3.8. If $\delta = 0$, which corresponds to the perfect mobility of capital, then $r_e = r_{a2}$ which is the case where there is no technological change. With any amount of technological change, the degree of capital mobility will be less than perfect working against the tendency of the equalization of profit rates of the Marxians and neoclassicals.

This example conveys the importance of the operationalization of the competition concept in terms of firms' investment behaviour and technological change. Firms, in order to preserve their initial investment, continuously invest in their fixed capital. The existence of fixed capital limits the firms' choice. As long as the profit rate in the industry is high enough to permit firms to preserve the competitiveness of their fixed capital they will stay in the industry, even though profit rates in the industry might be low relative to other industries.

What changes from one industry to another are the conditions to preserve the competitiveness of the fixed capital in each industry. These conditions are determined by competition at the industry level which also embodies the industry's technological and structural characteristics (as argued above). The rate of return required to preserve fixed capital in the textiles industry may be low, and the rate of return required to keep fixed capital competitive in the computer industry may be high, reflecting the differences in their technological dynamics. In both industries, the rate of return to keep fixed capital competitive will be driven to its minimum through competition. As long as firms are able to survive in the textile industry, they will have a preference for that industry because they are familiar with it. There is no reason to assume that the capital will flow from the textiles industry to the computer industry because of a higher rate of return to keep fixed capital competitive in the computer industry. Capital mobility will occur if the rate of return in an industry is higher than the rate of return necessary to keep fixed capital competitive. Otherwise, one needs to explain why the firms have been operating in the low-rate-of-return industries for decades. As shown in Table 3.3, the rate of return in the primary metals industries has been around 3–3.5 per cent, and 5–5.5% in textiles and paper, while 10 per cent in electric machines and 12–13 per cent in the motor vehicles industry for last three decades.

The persistence of the non-uniformity of profit rates shows the inappropriateness of the equilibrium framework in analysing capitalist economies. What characterizes capitalist economies is a continuous adjustment process rather than a movement towards a certain equilibrium. Continuous adjustment is provoked by firms' survival struggle as reflected in their investment behaviour. As survival conditions in an industry change, the required rate of return to preserve the competitiveness of fixed capital changes. The meaning of the prevailing profit rate in an industry should be evaluated in relation to the survival struggle in that industry. Basing the analysis on an artificially constructed equilibrium distorts the reality that we are supposed to understand and explain.

CONCLUSIONS

The conceptualization of competition as a survival process captures the fundamental features of the working of a capitalist economy: a continuous adjustment process, technological change, investment efforts, the institutional structure of an economy, relations between firms' pricing, investment and financing decisions, and the non-uniformity of profit rates. Uncertainty, present in all economic activities, is reflected in firms' behaviour rather than being assumed away by the knowledge of probability distributions. History does matter because the survival struggle of firms is specific to the institutional structure of an economy, and to the stage of industry which are both history specific.

The analytical power of any conceptual framework depends on its ability in lending itself to the analysis of basic economic issues. The conception of competition as a survival process can provide the basis for an analysis of basic economic issues. It gives a consistent explanation for the non-uniformity of profit rates which are swept under the carpet by the neoclassical and Marxist frameworks. It permits the analysis of firms' pricing behaviour together with investment and financing decisions in the post-Keynesian fashion *à la* Eichner (Chapter 5 presents econometric evidence for 'profit targeting' behaviour based on such a post-Keynesian pricing model).

Again, it is possible to explain why firms do finance themselves through their internal funds in the UK and the USA, whereas in Japan, Germany and other European countries they depend on bank borrowing (Chapter 6). These are initial attempts to analyse firms' pricing and financing behaviour using the conception of competition as a survival process.

NOTES

1. In a recent article, Nikaido explores the tendency for market prices to converge to the prices of production through capital mobility. Capital moves across sectors exclusively in pursuit of a higher profit rate without any other motivations, accompanied by the necessarily resulting net investments. He shows that, in the process of capital movement motivated by profit-seeking, the equalization of rates of profit is not a universal tendency but a phenomenon conditional on such a causal property of technology as the organic composition of the capital-goods sector relative to that of the consumption sector. In particular, the non-equalization of profit rates always prevails if the capital-goods sector has a higher organic composition, the situation which is often presumed in the Marxist view. He concludes that:

   Thus the result of our examination seems to suggest that prices of production are not natural prices to which market prices tend to be attracted, but just normative construction, an attribute of the social relation of production, like labor values. (Nikaido 1983: 362)

2. Recent studies have shown a high sensitivity of the prices of production to a very small change in the structure of production. Semmler (1984a, 1984b) carries out a sensitivity analysis and shows that prices of production can change in response to a small change in the structure of production:

This brings up again the problem of an economic adjustment process that could provide that the new production prices serve as centers of gravity for market prices. If linear production models for prices of production can reveal for certain matrices such properties of unstable solutions – as they did for certain value systems – and the economic adjustment processes do not exist, this would not allow the new production coefficients of the economy to determine the regulating production prices. Therefore, we can conclude again that in certain cases the equilibrium solution of the new production price system might not provide us with a very relevant determination of the long-run prices of production. (Semmler 1984a, 33)

Semmler adds that Marx himself seemed to have the view that neither values nor the general profit rate nor prices of production as the long-run centres of gravity change significantly when there are short-run and small changes in the input–output relations of industries or in the allocation of capital among industries.

3. However, it has been a consistent one from early on, as a letter from Ricardo to Malthus indicates:

Political Economy you think is an enquiry into the nature and causes of wealth. I think it should rather be called an enquiry into the laws which determine the division of the produce of industry amongst the classes who concur in its formation . . . Every day I am more satisfied that the former enquiry is vain and delusive, and the latter only the true object of science. Quoted in McNulty (1968) from *Work and Correspondence*, Vol. 8, ed. Piero Sraffa (Cambridge University Press: Cambridge, 1958: 278).

4. For similar remarks also see Nelson and Winter (1982: 45–8).
5. Some neoclassical economists acknowledge the importance of these inter-relationships. For example, in commenting on recent developments in game-theoretical approaches, Kreps and Spence conclude that:

competition in reality is over many variables or in many dimensions at once. These analyses are extremely useful in focusing our attention on the nature of competition in a single variable, but one wonders whether the nature of competition in one variable is not affected by what is happening with regard to a second. In other words, what are the 'general equilibrium' considerations of competition over these variables? (Kreps and Spence 1983: 15).

6. Langlois (ed.) (1986: 12) expresses similar views.
7. Farjoun and Machover (1983) present data for the UK manufacturing industries which show the non-uniformity of profit rates.

4. A Model of Firm Behaviour

THE SETTING

The environment in which firms operate in market economies can be described by relations at five different levels:

- between firms within industries
- between firms across industries
- between firms and financial institutions
- between firms and workers
- between firms and the state.

The interaction among these levels form the competitive process. The last three essentially reflect the institutional structure of the economy. In this chapter we concentrate on the interactions among the first three levels.

By competitive process I mean rivalry among firms not only in price dimension but also in investment which generates advances in technology. Investment is an integral part of competition because it enables firms to survive successfully in the coming periods. To survive, firms need to produce at minimum costs established in that period. Failing to do so means losing their market share and eventually disappearance from the market altogether. To reduce costs, firms invest continuously.

The need for investment implies the need for financial funds, whose availability and conditions are determined on the financial markets. There is thus a close link between the intensity of the competitive struggle among firms and the financial structure of the economy. By favouring or not favouring some firms relative to others, the financial structure of the economy will affect the competitive process in the economy. It is not possible to analyse this process without taking its interaction with the financial markets into consideration. The assumptions about the institutional structure of the economy need to be made explicit.

In the model below, I assume a securities-based financial system in which firms have direct access to loanable funds as long as they provide profitable alternatives for the investors. In such a system, banks are independent from industrial firms. Industrial firms and banks are not in a close relationship through either joint ownership, directorship or state intervention at the expense of third-party industrial firms, and the credit-rationing criteria of banks are based on the profitability of loans for the banks. The existence of financial institutions independent from industrial firms intensifies the competition between firms by making lending possible to firms which may otherwise be competed out if without access to funds.

DETERMINATION OF THE INTERNAL FINANCING RATIO

The most important decision in the investment process is firms' investment in physical capital. The fixed nature of physical capital extends firms' horizon beyond the short run. In the short run, firms can not recover their fixed capital costs; their capital is immobilized. It is, then, reasonable to argue that firms commit themselves for a long period when they make a decision to invest in an industry and consequently are interested in the long run maximization of profits. In the long run, uncertainty becomes the most important variable for firm behaviour. Firms do not know certain parameters, such as demand curves, and cannot predict competitors' plans for investment and technological change. In this context, market share becomes a strategic objective because it provides a means of insurance against uncertainty, it shows the relative performance of the firms. Losing market share is an indicator of the firm losing its competitive edge and failing to maximize profits relative to other firms. In addition, firms will be better off by expanding their market share to the point of diseconomies. Mueller (1986) found that more efficient firms earn higher profits and grow to be bigger than the less efficient firms in their industries. Of the firms that had persistently high profits in Mueller's sample of the 1000 largest manufacturing firms as of 1950, many were dominant companies in their markets. An increase in market share provides opportunities for economies of scale in production, marketing, R&D expenditures and market power.

The role of market share in providing a means of insurance against uncertainty in a dynamic context was recognized by earlier writers. Harrod observed its importance in his *Economic Essays* (1952):

All entrepreneurs ... have in mind the vast uncertainties of a relatively distant future. The best method of insuring against them is to attach to oneself by ties of goodwill as large a market as possible as quickly as possible. If one can get a substantially larger market by earning no more than a normal profit than one could get by earning a surplus profit ... one may well choose to do the former, as an insurance against future uncertainties.[1]

Heflebower had similar observations in his article 'Toward a Theory of Industrial Markets and Prices' (1954):

Management recognizes good market position to be a valuable asset, whose long-term attributes must condition all short-term decisions. Its value is not merely defensive ... but also is a basic attribute of the firm's ability to make positive moves; that is, to deal with unanticipated developments when they occur. In that sense, market position becomes a means of long-term profit maximization under conditions of uncertainty.[2]

In order to secure their market share and expand it, firms need to invest. Firms invest either to keep up by increasing demand, to reduce costs or to produce new and better products. Any other way of expanding depends on the availability of investable funds.

The need for funds becomes crucial for firms' pricing decisions because through pricing they can affect their profits, which may provide the basic source of investable funds. The importance of profits as the basic source of funds for investment arises because the investment process is determined by the competitive process. To stay competitive, firms may undertake some projects with a rate of return less than the cost of borrowing. This implies that the investment is no longer a unique function of the rate of return as the marginal efficiency of investment theory or the neo-classical investment theories suggest. Conventional theories of investment also assume that firms are perfectly competitive, thus prices are data for firms in the evaluation of investment projects. However, if firms are able to set the prices, they can change the rate of return on their investments.

The nature of the investment process is not given due consideration in conventional theories of investment. It is assumed that the investment-project space is determined by individual firms, that is, firms decide to undertake investment projects without regard to the actions of other firms. It is a well-observed fact that firms keep a close eye on their competitors' investment plans so as not to fall behind in competition. If a project is going to provide a cost advantage to the firm undertaking the investment, then similar investment projects will be undertaken by other firms in the industry. The investment-project space, in that case, is determined by the competitive process.

The competitive process is largely shaped by the financial structure of the economy. Credit-based financial systems differ from securities-based financial systems in determining the availability and conditions of finance (see Chapter 6). In this chapter, the existence of a securities-based financial system is assumed.

In securities-based financial systems, firms raise funds in the capital market through the issuance of bonds and stocks. Thus funds come directly from the savings units in the economy, independent of the influence of financial intermediaries. The relationship between the firms and the financial intermediaries is limited since the ultimate choice of investment is determined by the investor. In such systems, potential entrants have access to investable funds as long as they present a profitable asset for investors' portfolios. This requires that they show a profitable alternative to the incumbent firms in terms of return and risk. This is possible only if new entrants are at least as efficient as existing firms in technological innovation, cost structure and the ability to produce better-quality products. These conditions constitute a list of minimum requirements for entry.

The availability of funds to new entrants induces existing firms to rely on internal funds given the fact that potentially successful challenges from new entrants may reduce the possibility of raising funds in the capital markets. Exit from financial holdings is easy through well-developed secondary markets. In troubled times, investors will dispose of the securities of the existing firms in favour of successful new entrants, making it very difficult for incumbent firms to obtain funds when the funds are most needed. Banks will abstain from getting into long-term relationships with firms because banks are vulnerable to the same forces in the presence of well-developed capital markets.

Two factors are important in the determination of the internal financing ratio in the approach presented above: the competitive nature of the investment process, and the institutional structure of the financial system as reflected in the availability of capital to new entrants and the possibilities of exit for lenders.

Let's assume that there are two firms in the industry: Firm A and Firm B, and entry into the industry is a function of average profitability π_i. Where

$\pi_i = \bigcap_i / \gamma_i$	= average profitability in the industry in period i
$\bigcap_i$	= profits in the industry in period i
γ_i	= sales in the industry in period i
$r_{ij} = \bigcap_{ij} / K_{ij}$	= the rate of return for firm j in period i
$\bigcap_{ij}$	= profits in period i for firm j
K_{ij}	= capital stock of firm j in period i
i	= 1, 2 $j = A, B$
r_c	= the rental cost of capital for periods 1 and 2

If we start from an equilibrium position in the industry in period 1, we have

$$r_{1A} = r_{1B} = r_c$$

and the prices are set at a level that, given the quantity of output, there is no entry into the industry. It is assumed that the total quantity demanded stays constant. The firms' objective is assumed to be long-run competitiveness or survival. This is a post-Keynesian objective (Eichner 1976, Wood 1975) which takes into account the fixed nature of physical capital.

Conventional theories of investment suggest that firms will undertake investment only if the rate of return on additional investment is where $r_{2j} \geq r_c$. Let's assume then that investment project I, if taken by only one firm, will yield a rate of return higher than the cost of borrowing of capital, that is $r_{2j} \geq r_c$. $R_{2j} \geq r_c$ because the investment project provides a cost advantage for the firm undertaking it and enables the firm to reduce the price and to squeeze the profits and market share of other firms so as not to cause entry into the industry. Otherwise, if the firm does not reduce the price, the average profitability in the industry will rise, inducing the entry of new firms. For simplicity, assume that Firm B's profits will be zero if Firm A undertakes the investment and B does not undertake it, or vice versa.

Thus, we have the following situation:

A \ B	Undertakes investment	Does not undertake investment
Undertakes investment	r_{2AB}	$r_{2A}, 0$
Does not undertake investment	$0, r_{2B}$	$r_{1A} = r_{1B} = r_c$

Where r_{2AB} = the rate of return if both firms undertake the investment project.

From Firm A's *ex-ante* point of view, if Firm B undertakes the investment, and Firm A does not undertake it, Firm A's rate of return will be 0. If Firm A undertakes the investment, its rate of return will be r_{2AB}. Thus, Firm A will undertake the investment if Firm B undertakes it. In the case of Firm B not undertaking the investment, if Firm A does not undertake it, Firm A's rate of return will be $r_{1A} = r_c$. If Firm A undertakes the investment, Firm A's return will be r_{2a} which is greater than $r_{1A} = r_c$. That is, Firm A will undertake the investment even if Firm B does not undertake it.

Since $r_{2AB} > 0$ and $r_{2A} = r_{2B} > r_c$, undertaking the investment will be the dominant strategy and both firms will undertake it. Undertaking the investment is the dominant strategy because the possibility of entry prevents collusion among the existing firms. If firms collude and do not undertake the investment, the opportunity may be captured by a potential entrant. Such an entry satisfies the entry conditions of cost efficiency. The assumption of well-developed capital markets provides the capital needed for entry.

If both firms undertake the investment, the rate of return that will prevail in the second period is r_{2AB}. Note that the firms will undertake the investment even if $r_{2AB} < r_c$ as long as $r_{2AB} > 0$. The comparison of r_{2AB} with r_c does not enter the investment decision-making process at all when the investment space is determined by the competitive process,[3] and access to capital is possible to new entrants through the well-developed capital markets. Baumol *et al.* (1970, 1973) present empirical evidence for the result derived from the simple model above that the firms may invest in projects with a rate of return less than the cost of borrowing. They analysed the rates of return on investments financed by internal funds, debt and equity for the period 1946–66 for 900 firms. They found that the rate of return on internal funds ranges from 3.0 to 4.6 per cent, on debt from 4.2 per cent to 14 per cent and on newly issued equity from 14 to 21 per cent. In a second study, to respond to criticisms made against their 1970 study, the authors found that for firms which issued no significant amount of new equity the average rate of return on internal funds was in the neighbourhood of 0.

Mobility out of the industry is restricted because of the

fixed nature of physical capital in the short run and firms' commitment to long-run competitiveness. The existence of fixed capital and long-run competitiveness, or the survival objective, implies that the insider–outsider distinction of neoclassical economics loses its importance. If the firm does not undertake the investment it will not be able to generate cash flows due to its loss of competitiveness. The value of the firm will depreciate. If stockholders decide to transfer their stocks, they will do so at a substantial loss. From the stockholders' point of view, fixed capital is a sunk cost. From the managers' point of view, if they do not secure the competitiveness of their firms, their credibility will suffer. It is in the interest of both the stockholders and the managers to take a long-term view of competition and promote their common interests.[4] In a recent article, Baden-Fuller (1989), who analysed the process of exit from the steel-casting industry, found that firms which were diversified and financially strong seemed more likely to close than those which were not, and speculates that in these firms there may have been fewer conflicts between the various stakeholders: owners, debtholders and managers.

Returning to the financing decisions of firms, firms face real uncertainty in the Knightian sense. They do not know and cannot estimate the probabilities of the amount and time of the investment projects that may have a rate of return which is less than the cost of borrowing capital. This implies that they continuously need to rely on a source of finance that will assure the availability of funds. The possibility that the rate of return on some investment projects may be less than the cost of capital rules out the capital markets as the main source of funds for firm's investments. Capital markets will not provide funds for investments that may have low rates of return but which are crucial for the competitiveness of firms. In the securities-based systems, internal funds are the main source of finance that firms can exercise control over to undertake investment projects that are crucial for their competitiveness.

Internal funds are supplied by two sources: profits and depreciation allowances. Since depreciation allowances are determined by tax laws and past capital expenditures, firms can obtain larger amounts of internal funds by increasing profits, which can be secured by raising the price of the product sold. Higher prices imply a decline in future revenues due to higher demand elasticity in the long run and to new entry caused by rising prices. In this way, one can calculate the implicit cost of internal funds as Eichner (1976) suggests. However, internal funds have two advantages over external funds that qualify them as the main source of finance in the context of the above analysis: firms have control over internal funds through their pricing decisions; and the cost of internal funds accrues in the future without imposing constraints on firms' current investment behaviour which is crucial for firms' near-future competitiveness. The size of the negative impact of raising internal funds through price increases is unknown since this impact will accrue through overtime. Firms do not even know the current demand curve they face. One cannot assume that they base their calculations on future demand curves. However, the negative impact of not undertaking investment to maintain competitiveness is known with certainty – loss of market share in the immediate future.

This does not imply that firms will persistently be undertaking investment projects with rates of return less than the opportunity cost of capital. It shows that firms understand the fact that in the competitive struggle, they may be forced to undertake some investment projects with rates of return less than the cost of borrowing. It is the existence of such a possibility pointed out by the simple model above and empirical evidence that firms have to consider in order not to endanger their long-run survival by short-run credit squeezes. Otherwise, the profitability of investment projects is important for the long-run survival of firms.

THE JOINT DETERMINATION OF PRICE AND THE INTERNAL FINANCING RATIO

The determination of internal financing ratios can be explained using graphs which take into account the cost of increasing the ratio of internal funds (IF) to investments (I) to the benefit of increasing the IF/I ratio. This also provides an

Figure 4.1

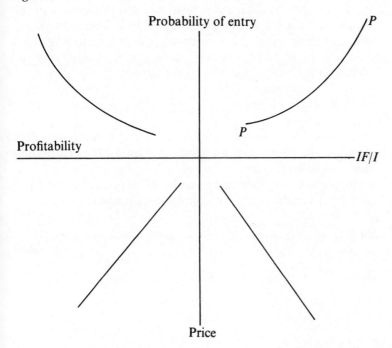

analysis of joint determination of price and internal financing ratio.

Under uncertainty, firms do not know and cannot estimate the probabilities of the amount and time of the investment projects that may have a rate of return which is less than the cost of borrowing capital. The best firms can do is to set prices at a level that will equate the cost of increasing the ratio of *IF/I* to the benefit of increasing the *IF/I* ratio.

The cost of increasing the internal financing ratio is the increase in the probability of entry into the industry. Firms increase the *IF/I* ratio through increasing prices (Quadrant IV, Figure 4.1). An increase in prices, given the costs, implies an increase in the profitability of the industry (Quadrant III, Figure 4.1).

As the profitability of the industry increases, the probability of entry will increase. The probability of entry will increase at an increasing rate because relatively more firms will be induced to enter (Quadrant II, Figure 4.1). The relationship between the profitability of entry and the *IF/I* ratio is referred to as 'the probability function' since the profitability of the industry increases as the *IF/I* ratio increases:

$$\text{Probability of entry } (PE) = p(IF/I) \qquad (4.1)$$

where $dp/dIF/I > 0$ and $d^2p/dIF^2/I > 0$ implying that as *IF/I* increases the probability of entry increases at an increasing rate (Figure 4.1).

The profitability function can also be expressed in terms of the rate of return, using the definition of profitability:

$$\frac{\pi}{Y} = \frac{\pi}{K} \times \frac{K}{Y} \qquad (4.2)$$

where

π = profits
Y = sales
K = capital

Given the capital-output ratio, there is a direct relationship between the rate of return realized in the industry and the *IF/I* ratio. This relationship is derived in Figure 4.2.

The profitability function explains only one half of entry, and it is the only one that is accounted for in the limit-entry models (see Scherer 1980, Sawyer 1979). The other half of entry is related to the source of funds available for entry. Limit-pricing models state that as the profitability in the industry increases, firms will enter the industry but do not discuss whether at the given level of profitability funds will be available to potential entrants to make entry possible. Limit-pricing models, then, implicitly assume that the funds will be available to firms at any profitability level that firms want to enter the industry. However, this is assuming away the problem since the availability of funds to the industry is

Figure 4.2

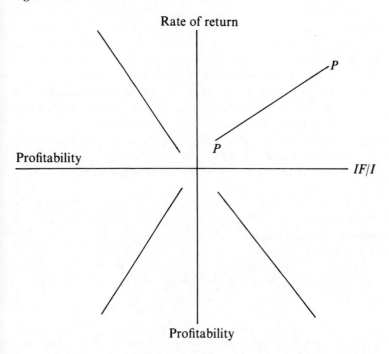

dependent upon the profitability in the industry. Limit-pricing models will become theoretically complete and meaningful only when the available funds constraint is taken into account.

The benefit of increasing the *IF/I* ratio, on the other hand, is that it provides a barrier to entry by reducing the expected rate of return in the industry. It should already be clear that as the possibility of the rate of return on investment falling below the cost of borrowing increases, firms will want to increase the *IF/I* ratio so as to finance the higher share of investments through internal funds and not go bankrupt. That is, by changing the internal financing ratio, firms may convey information about the expected rate of return on investment in the industry. Let's assume that financial lenders form expectations about the rate of return on investment in the industry as follows:

$$r_e = \alpha \, r_L + (1 - \alpha) \, r_H \qquad (4.3)$$

where

α $= IF/I$
r_e $=$ expected rate of return
r_L $=$ lower bound on the rate of return on investment which
     may be less than cost of borrowing as occurs in the case
     when firms fully pass on the cost reductions
r_H $=$ the upper bound on the rate of return on investment
     which is higher than the cost of borrowing as is the case
     when firms do not pass on the cost reductions

Given r_H, and r_L by changing α, firms can manipulate the expectations of financial lenders as to the rate of return in the industry. This is entirely plausible since the financial lenders will assume that firms are in the best situation to judge the possibilities of the return on investment in the industry. Firms face bankruptcy or loss if they underestimate the possibility of the rate of return on the investment being less than the rental cost of borrowing capital. On the other hand, if firms overestimate the possibility of the rate of return being less than the rental cost of capital, they help to prevent entry by lowering the expected rate of return. This relationship is derived in Figure 4.3. As the *IF/I* ratio increases, the expected rate of return declines as given by equation 3 (Quadrant IV, Figure 4.3).

Loanable funds to the industry increase with an increase in the expected rate of return on capital in the industry (Quadrant III, Figure 4.3). There are two reasons behind this positive relationship: as the firms' borrowing needs increase relative to their own invested capital, lenders charge higher risk premiums (this is Kalecki's (1937) 'principle of increasing risk'); since the loanable funds in the economy are not unlimited, they become more available with an increase in the expected rate of return on capital in an industry.

The probability of entry also increases with the increase in loanable funds to the industry (Quadrant II, Figure 4.3). That is, as the *IF/I* ratio increases, the probability of entry to the

Figure 4.3

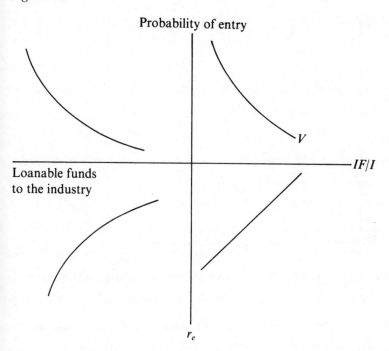

industry declines (Quadrant I, Figure 4.3). This relationship is called the 'vulnerability function' because as the IF/I ratio increases, firms become less vulnerable to entry. The vulnerability function is then

$$PE = v\,(IF/I) \tag{4.4}$$

with $dv/dIF/I < 0$ and $d^2v/d\,IF^2/I > 0$, meaning that as the IF/I ratio increases, the expected rate of return declines at an increasing rate (Figure 4.3).

The vulnerability curve can also be presented in terms of the rate of return and the IF/I ratio, as shown in Figure 4.4.

The target ratio of IF/I will be determined by the intersection of the profitability and vulnerability curves. The adjustment process in the firms' decision-making process can be

Figure 4.4

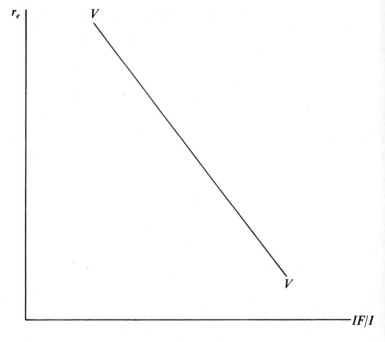

described as follows: the vulnerability curve gives the expected rate of return (r_e) on investment for a given level of the IF/I ratio. The profitability curve gives the rate of return that will actually be realized (r_r) for the given IF/I ratio. This is because $\pi/Y = \pi/K \cdot K/Y$ and the K/Y is constant along the profitability curve.

Firms choose a point on the vulnerability curve. By choosing an IF/I ratio, firms will affect the expected rate of return on investment in the industry, which determines the availability of loans to the industry. A firm's ability to determine the expected rate of return by setting the α gives rise to a 'moral hazard'. It is in the interest of existing firms to keep the expected rate of return as low as possible by increasing the α if they want to reduce the availability of loanable funds to new entrants or increase the expected rate of return whenever they

Figure 4.5

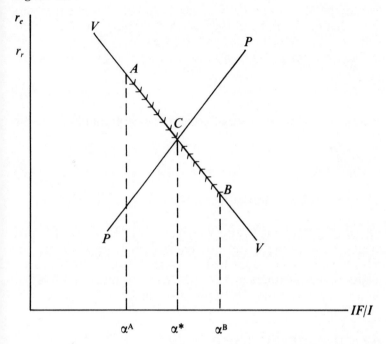

themselves demand additional funds from the financial markets. That is, existing firms have the incentive to overstate the α so as to keep entry at a minimum, and understate the α so as to obtain additional funds. However, the moral-hazard problem arising from the firm's ability to set α is counteracted because the credibility of firms will be assured only when $r_e = r_r$.

For example, at point A the expected rate of return is higher than the rate of return that will be realized at that point. Firms not only increase uncertainty in their relationships with the financial markets because of miscalculating the rate of return, but actually lose money on the basis of their expectations. So firms will increase the α^A to α^* where $r_e = r_r$. Incumbent firms cannot sustain point B either, because they are losing credibility at point B. The rate of return that will be realized at point *B* is higher than the expected rate of return suggested by the choice of α revealing their desire to reduce the entry into the industry. To prevent the loss of credibility and entry that will result, firms will reduce α^B to α^* where $r_e = r_r$.

The firms' target *IF/I* ratio is, then, at point C where

$$r_e = r_r \tag{4.5}$$

and the adjustment process in firms' decision making process is

$$\dot{\alpha} = f(r_e - r_r) \tag{4.6}$$

where $\dot{\alpha}$ = change in the *IF/I* ratio

Firms target the *IF/I* ratio where $r_e = r_r$. However, if firms' demand expectations are not realized, the expected rate of return will not be equal to the realized rate of return. This leads to an adjustment process which can be understood in the context of the pricing decisions of the firms.

PRICING BEHAVIOUR

The pricing behaviour of firms can be described as profit-targeting. Firms, on the basis of their investment decisions, target their profits so as to provide the internal funds needed to finance the investment expenditures which are essential for their survival. Firms base their pricing decisions on cost and investment expenditures, about both of which firms have hard knowledge.[5] It is not assumed that firms know their demand curve, nor is it necessary to make such a strong assumption. Even if firms know the demand curve they are facing, they would not charge a price lower than the one suggested by the profit-targeting behaviour as that would endanger their survival, nor could they charge a price higher than the profit-targeting one as it would induce entry.

Profit-targeting behaviour, thus, hits Friedman's famous defence of profit maximization at its heart. Friedman argued that:

unless the behavior of businessmen in some way or other approximated behavior consistent with the maximization of returns, it seems unlikely that they would remain in business for long. Let the apparent, immediate determinant of business behavior be anything at all – habitual reaction, random chance or whatnot. Whenever this determinant happens to lead to behavior consistent with the rational and informed maximization of returns, the business will prosper and acquire resources with which to expand; whenever it does not, the business will tend to lose resources and can be kept in existence only by the addition of resources from outside. The process of 'natural selection' thus helps to validate the hypothesis – or, rather, given natural selection, acceptance of the hypothesis can be based largely on the judgement that it summarizes appropriately the conditions for survival. (1953: 22)

Profit-targeting behaviour, not the profit maximization of neoclassicals, assures the survival of firms. Prices lower than suggested by such behaviour endanger the survival of firms because they will not obtain the investment funds necessary to survive in the future through profits. In a similar fashion, prices above the profit-targeting will make survival difficult for firms by inducing entry into the industry.

Investments and related factors such as uncertainty and ignorance form the basis of profit-targeting behaviour and are crucial for survival. This is what is lacking in the profit-maximization postulate. As Koopmans commented on Friedman's defence:

A postulate about individual behavior is made more plausible by making reference to the adverse effects of, and hence the penalty for, departures from the postulated behavior. The reality of the penalty is documented by technological and institutional facts, such as reproductability of production processes and the operation of accounting procedures in bankruptcy laws, facts which are a degree less elusive to verification than mere behavioral postulates. But if this is the basis for our belief in profit maximization, then we should postulate that basis itself and not the profit maximization which it implies in certain circumstances. (1957: 140)

Profit-targeting behaviour reflects firms' response to uncertainty. Their knowledge of demand is limited. The only knowledge they can claim is about their cost structures. Firms' investment decisions are based upon their calculation of the minimum amount of investment needed to stay competitive. Such decisions are also made in response to firms' lack of knowledge about their rivals' behaviour. Under these circumstances, prices are determined by their investment decisions over their costs.

Investment decisions are instrumental in affecting the determination of demand expectations. Firms' investment decisions depend on some expectations of demand in the future. All the empirical studies on investment show that output is the most important explanatory variable.[6] In a dynamic context, then, the price–output decision is not a simultaneous one as would be suggested by knowledge of the demand curve, but a sequential one. Firms undertake investment in this period with some expectations of demand for the next period. In the next period, firms' output-level expectations have already been embodied in their investment decisions of this period.

Given the above discussion, the pricing behaviour of firms can be formalized. Schematically, the importance of pricing decisions in a long-run perspective can be shown as:

Long-run maximization of profits → Long-run strategy
of securing market shares → Dynamic competition →
Investment decisions → Pricing behaviour (profit-targeting)

Firms' pricing decisions need to be considered along with a long-run strategy of keeping market shares, that is, satisfying the firms' need for funds to undertake investments which firms see as essential for their competitiveness. While securing their market share requires pricing behaviour that will limit entry, the need for funds for investments to stay competitive in a dynamic context requires prices high enough at least to provide funds to undertake investments. That is, short-run pricing behaviour must reconcile seemingly contradictory strategies of securing market shares both in the short and long runs.

I assume, first, that the price norm for the industry will be set at the average efficiency (representative firm) level by the most efficient firm, or the price leader. This is a familiar assumption in many models, including those of Andrews,

Downie, Eichner and Steindl, among other post-Keynesians, which is based on the results of industry studies carried out by these researches. If there are efficiency differences across the firms in the industry, as one would expect, these will be reflected in varying profitability, growth and the capital structures of the firms. For example, less efficient firms will borrow more to undertake investments in order to stay competitive relative to more efficient firms. Since the price level is set at the representative firm level, we will observe a distribution of firms with different IF/I ratios in the industry.

Second, I assume that in the relevant range of output, marginal costs will be constant. The theoretical justification for this assumption comes from the fact that under uncertainty, capacity utilization becomes a choice variable.[7] Firms can adjust to demand conditions in the short run by changing the capacity-utilization rate. Operating at less than full capacity gives firms a safety margin against their rivals. Smith (1969) has shown that under conditions of uncertainty, a monopoly will attempt to operate its plant, on average, below the full capacity rate. This will be more true under an oligopolistic market structure because firms will not want to be caught unprepared against demand shocks; what is at stake is their market shares. Empirically, capacity utilization in the manufacturing industries has been around 83 per cent in the post-World War II period.[8] If the firms underutilize their productive capacity, we can assume that in the relevant range firms can change their output without changing their marginal costs.[9]

Given its productive capacity, expected demand level and perception of the amount of investment needed, the most efficient firm will set the price at a level that will provide funds to undertake investments. In other words, firms target their profits. The profit-targeting behaviour of firms can be formalized as follows:

$$\pi_r = P_i Q_{ei} - \Sigma b_{ji} Q_{ei} - CCA_r \qquad (4.7)$$

π_r = profits of the representative firm
P_i = price of the ith commodity
Q_{ei} = expected demand level

b_{ji} = fixed input coefficients
CCA_r = capital consumption allowances

Firms' target profits are determined by their investment and dividend decisions. There are two internal sources that firms use to finance investment and dividend expenditures: profits and capital consumption allowances. If α is less than one, then some portion of the investment will be financed from external sources through debt or new equity issues.

$$\pi_r + CCA_r = \alpha I_r + D_r \qquad (4.8)$$

where

I_r = investment decisions taken at the beginning of the period t for period $t+1$
D_r = dividends firms expect to pay

We have already discussed the determination of α (see pp. 76–84). I assume that the dividend–payout ratio (β) is exogenously determined, following the finance literature since Lintner's seminal article (1956), which found that firms have a target – payout ratio which is a constant proportion of their internal funds. That is,

$$\beta = \frac{D_r}{\pi_r + CCA_r} \qquad (4.9)$$

or

$$D_r = \beta \, (\pi_r + CCA_r) \qquad (4.10)$$

β is a less traditional measure of a target–payout ratio than the dividend/after-tax profit ratio used in the finance literature. This is justified on both theoretical and empirical grounds. Theoretically, β is closer to the spirit of a stable target – payout ratio of the Lintner tradition because capital consumption allowances show a less fluctuating trend than after tax profits. This is because capital consumption allowances are less cyclical than after tax profits. In addition, capital consumption allowances embody firms' past growth efforts which should be reflected in stockholder dividend payments, since the undistributed profits of the past have been used to finance the expansion of the capital stock. Empirically, the target – payout ratio based on profits plus capital consumption allowances shows very little variance to the one based on after-tax profits.[10]

It is reasonable to start with the assumption that firms know their capital consumption allowances with certainty and first satisfy the needs of funds for investment rather than dividends because investment is crucial for their survival and thus their ability to pay dividends in the future.

$$\alpha I_r - CCA_r = \varkappa I_r \tag{4.11}$$

$\varkappa I_r$ = the portion of the investment that needs to be financed out of profits

$$\varkappa I_r = \pi_r - \beta (\pi_r + CCA_r) \tag{4.12}$$

If we solve (4.12) for π_r

$$\pi_r = \frac{\varkappa I_r + \beta\, CCA_r}{1 - \beta} \tag{4.13}$$

Solve for $CCA_r + \pi_r$ from (4.11) and (4.13)

$$CCA_r + \pi_r = \alpha I_r - \varkappa I_r + \frac{\varkappa I_r + \beta\, CCA_r}{1 - \beta} \tag{4.14}$$

Simplifying (4.14)

$$CCA_r + \pi_r = \frac{\alpha}{1 - \beta} I_r \tag{4.15}$$

Substituting (4.15) into (4.7) and solving for the price gives:

$$P_i = \Sigma b_{ji} p_j + \frac{\alpha}{1 - \beta} \cdot \frac{I_r}{Q_e} \tag{4.16}$$

As seen from equation (4.16), firms' pricing decisions depend

Figure 4.6

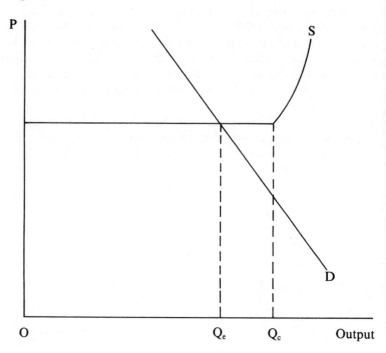

on their costs and investment decisions.

The basic theme of profit-targeting behaviour can be presented in the price–output space. In Figure 4.6, the firm's
supply curve is perfectly elastic at a price level determined by
the investment decisions on the basis of demand expectations
at Q_e until the capacity output level is reached. The supply
curve is drawn for a given expected output level. As the
expected output level changes, the supply curve shifts.

The expected output level is OQ_e. At this level of output the
firm determines its selling price on the basis of profit-targeting
behaviour. It follows that once the firm's costs of production,
investment decisions and demand expectations have been
specified, the firm's short-period output supply curve can be
described (the demand curve does not play any role in the

determination of price).

The expected rate of return is based on the expected level of demand. As this differs from the realized level of demand, the realized rate of return will differ from the expected rate of return. If the realized level of demand is less than the expected level, the realized rate of return will be less than the expected rate of return. The differences between the expected and realized rates of return will be transmitted to the financial market through changes in demand for investable funds. In this respect, the rate of return and output are positively correlated: as output increases, the realized rate of return increases.

If the investment decisions of firms differ, firms that expect to be able to compete with the least amount of investment will put competitive pressure on other firms, that is, competition is not only on price but also on investment and innovation. Since profit needs are determined by investment decisions and investment decisions depend on sectoral competition, the intensity of sectoral competition becomes important. This depends on the technological dynamics, the history of the industry and the growth rate of the demand for the industry's output. These three factors are inter-related and will differ from one industry to another. For example, in the computer industry where the turnover rate of fixed capital is high and technological innovation is rapid, the need for internal funds will be high. The history of the industry will include technological factors, the stability of demand growth and import competition. New industries may have higher needs for funds because of technological characteristics of the industry and the rapid growth of demand. Demand may have an ambiguous effect on investment decisions. If demand is increasing for the industry's output, firms will invest to expand capacity (the accelerator effect). However, at the same time, by providing more room for existing firms, demand growth may lessen the intensity of competition; or, as in the emergence of mini-plants in the steel industry, declining demand may intensify the competition at the sectoral level, promoting technological changes.

History also includes import competition because firms' response to such competition may depend on the lifecycle of the industry together with the availability of funds for such a response. For example, in a growing industry such as computers, firms may invest in new technologies that will increase their competitiveness in response to import competition. It may be relatively less difficult for firms in a growing industry to find external funds even though import competition reduces revenues through a profit squeeze. In a declining industry, such as steel, firms may hesitate to invest in new technologies to improve their relative position against imports, and may also have a hard time to convince financial lenders to finance investments in their industry.

Investment may be modelled as follows:

$$I = f[\dot{Q}, C \text{ (technological dynamics, history, } \dot{Q})] \qquad (4.17)$$

where

$\dot{Q}$ = the expected growth rate of demand
C = intensity of competition

and the partials are $\frac{\delta I}{\delta C} > 0, \frac{\delta I}{\delta Q} > 0$.

The profitability of industries depends on their competitive conditions as reflected in their investment decisions i.e. there will be° profitability differentials between industries. The mobility of capital may become effective if the profitability of some industries is high or perceived to be high relative to their competitive conditions.

Continuous adjustment is a permanent feature of the model. Firms are continuously undertaking investments which cause changes in technology and in the level of output.[11] If equilibrium has any meaning in this model, it can be defined as a situation where firms' profit targets are met. Even then, due to investments undertaken, equilibrium is changing continuously. The adjustment process does not move towards the earlier equilibrium which has not been reached but towards a new target which is different than the old one. In this context, equilibrium has no meaning.

If the profit targets of the firms are not met, the adjustment process that takes place may be analysed at two different levels, macro and micro. At the micro level, the adjustment is induced by the discrepancies between the expected and the realized output levels. If the output expectations of the firms are not realized, that will be reflected either in their pricing or investment decisions or in both in the following period. For a given level of investment, firms may raise their prices to increase internal funds to finance investment expenditures. If there are constraints on the firms' ability to raise prices either at the macro or micro levels, to continue to undertake the investments to which they are already committed would be to let their internal funds/investments (IF/I) ratios decline. The cyclical behaviour of the IF/I ratio will capture the adjustment process when there are constraints on the price setting ability of firms.

At the micro level, firms may face several price constraints. For example, price constraints may be due to the relative inefficiency revealed by competing imports or government intervention. In this case, import competition threatens the survival of firms, which respond by borrowing to invest and improve their competitive situation. Financial markets' evaluation of the riskiness of the firms becomes crucial for their future. For example, it would not be possible for the Chrysler Corporation to have borrowed heavily if the government had not intervened to bail it out. Intervention assured an increase in protectionism which would not have been taken for granted by the private lenders.

Government price intervention or import competition in declining industries impairs the profitability expectations of the firms. Our assumption was that firms set prices. Given output expectations, profitability expectations are formed in relation to the investments' contribution to the competitiveness of the firms. Government intervention or import competition imposes profitability expectations that may not be based on this competitiveness criterion. This may lead firms to rent-seeking behaviour rather than competitive improvements. For example, in the steel industry in the USA, rather than investing in the industry, firms have diversified into areas such as oil.

At the macro level, either of the following two situations is possible:

- total profits in the economy are enough to justify the planned investment needs of firms, but relative prices are not formed in a way that distributes the total profits in accordance with sectoral needs; and
- total profits in the economy are not enough to justify planned investment needs.

In the first case, a correction in relative prices is needed which may be brought about through price changes, entry, technological change that saves on inputs which have become expensive or intensified intra-industry competition that shifts market shares and may increase concentration. In the second case, if total profits are not enough to meet total investment needs, they may result in an inflationary spiral due to the firms' efforts to capture higher shares of total profits by raising prices. It should be noticed that the source of inflation in this model adds another dimension to the post-Keynesian inflation models. In those models, inflation results from distributional conflict between firms and workers; in the model developed here, inflation may result from the competitive struggle which involves both firms and industries.

SHIFTS IN THE PROFITABILITY AND VULNERABILITY CURVES

While the profitability reflects industry-specific characteristics, such as capital intensity, import competition and the growth rate of demand, the vulnerability curve is affected by institutional factors, such as the easiness of entry provided by the financial system. As these characteristics change from one industry to another, or one institutional setting to another, the observed IF/I ratios will be changing. Changes in the capital intensity of the industry and import competition will shift the profitability curve. Since the capital–output ratio is given along the profitability curve, any change in the capital–output ratio can be presented as a shift in the profitability curve. A lower capital intensity for a given profitability level implies that the rate of return in that industry is higher for a given IF/I ratio, implying that the new profitability curve lies above the old one.

Import competition restricts the ability of domestic firms to set prices. This reverses the causality relation that runs from the IF/I ratio to prices. The given price level in this context corresponds to a lower IF/I ratio. Import competition shifts the profitability curve to the left; import protection, on the other hand, shifts the profitability curve to the right.

The growth rate of output in the industry will affect the profitability curve to the extent that it changes π/Y for a given price. If π/Y is higher for a given price, the profitability curve will shift upwards and left. The profitability curves of high-growth industries will lie above the profitability curves of the slow-growth ones.

As the growth changes, one may expect that the gap between r_L and r_H to get larger as well as the absolute value of r_H. This is because there might be relatively more opportunities in growing industries. To the extent that the gap between r_L and r_H widens, the slope of the vulnerability curve gets steeper. A relatively flat vulnerability curve implies a higher IF/I ratio for a given r_H and a given profitability curve.

Capital intensity, import competition and growth rate are the variables that account for inter-industry differences in the internal financing ratios in a country. Industries with low capital intensity and a high growth rate will have a relatively lower internal financing ratio. We can restate the profitability equation so as to take into account these variables:

Probability of entry $(PE) = p(IF/I, K, M, Q)$ (4.18)

where

K = capital intensity of the industry
M = change in import competition
$\dot{Q}$ = growth rate of output

The vulnerability curve is determined by institutional

factors such as the type of existing financial system. Financial systems show differences from one country to another or through time in a country. The inter-country differences of internal financing ratios are, then, explained by movements in the vulnerability curve. Until now, the assumption about the financial markets was that they are independent from the industrial sector. This assumption is most accurate for the securities-based financial systems of the USA and UK. In these systems, the criterion for lending is the profitability of loans; as profitability increases, the amount of the loans made to that sector increases. We derived the downward-sloping vulnerability curve on the assumption of a securities-based financial system. If the financial system is credit based and credit is forthcoming to certain firms at a constant rate, we will have a relatively flat vulnerability curve. This implies that firms will rely on borrowing. Another implication is that since the lending rate does not clear the markets there will be credit rationing to new firms which will effectively prevent entry and this may sever the relationship between investment decisions and prices. This might be more true of the credit-based systems of developing countries than that of Germany and Japan. The impact of financial systems is analysed in Chapter 6.

NOTES

1. This quotation is from Scherer (1980: 235).
2. This quotation is from Scherer (1980: 265).
3. Scharfstein and Stein (1990) reach a similar conclusion in their herd-behaviour model.
4. See Brenner (1987: 8–11) for a similar view.
5. The distinction between hard and soft knowledge comes from Marglin and Bhaduri (1986).
6. See Jorgenson (1971) and Clark (1979) for a review of the literature.
7. See Lee *et al.* (1986: 18–24), Reynolds (1987: 77–8 and 1990: 239–42).
8. See the Economic Report of the President (1983).
9. For further discussion and empirical evidence see Eichner (1976).
10. Empirical evidence and discussion for this assumption can also be found in Brittain (1964, 1966), Turnovsky (1967) and Taggart (1984).
11. In this context the conceptual distinction between the short run and long run becomes blurred. For a similar remark see Lee (1984).

5. Econometric Evidence for US Manufacturing Industries

In this chapter, the hypotheses of the pricing model of the Chapter 4 are tested econometrically for the US manufacturing industries. There are two basic hypotheses that can be derived from the model: that the pricing behaviour of firms can be described as profit-targeting rather than profit-maximizing, which results from the conceptualization of competition as a survival process and reflects firms' attitude against uncertainty; and structural variables are significant in determining internal financing ratios within and across industries.

Empirical evidence for profit-targeting behaviour is presented. Empirical studies on alternative approaches such as profit maximization or sales maximization are reviewed to provide a comparison. The empirical evidence strongly supports profit-targeting behaviour, whereas profit-maximizing behaviour is refuted. The importance of the structural variables in the determination of internal financing ratios is tested using both time-series and cross-section analyses.

PROFIT-TARGETING BEHAVIOUR

The basic difference between profit-maximizing behaviour and profit-targeting behaviour, in an empirical sense, lies in the assumption made by profit-maximizing behaviour that firms know their demand curve. According to the profit-maximizing model, firms produce at the point where marginal revenue is equal to marginal cost. This implies that the profit-maximizing firm operates on the elastic portion of its demand curve. Profit-maximizing behaviour, then, can be tested by looking at the observed elasticity of the demand curve. Knowledge of the demand curve is not a relevant variable in profit-targeting behaviour. This results from the dynamic nature of such behaviour. Firms' demand expectations are embodied in their investment decisions. In this context, the investment decisions of firms become the most important variable. Given their costs of production, firms determine the prices with respect to their investment requirements. The testing of profit-targeting behaviour is possible by constructing a price variable based on such behaviour that can be regressed against actual prices. If the profit-targeting behaviour hypothesis is true, the coefficient of the constructed price variable should be equal to unity.

Tests of profit- and sales-maximizing behaviour have been done most recently by Koutsoyiannis (1984). Koutsoyiannis develops a theoretical framework which shows that an analysis of firm price elasticities of demand provides evidence about firm behaviour, since values less than one refute the profit-maximization and sales-maximization hypotheses, while providing support for Bain-type limit pricing. Koutsoyiannis derives a general relationship between market elasticity and firm elasticity of demand, which allows for an explicit treatment of the conjectural variations of firms. He then uses this relationship to infer firm behaviour from market elasticities for a group of 58 US four-digit industries over the 23-year period 1958–80 which corresponds to the time period of this study. He tests the estimated market elasticities for 54 industries against the null hypothesis of a unitary elasticity. In all cases, he finds that the price elasticity was not significantly greater than unity. More importantly, 95 per cent confidence intervals showed that for 37 industries, the price elasticity was smaller than unity, while for the remaining 17 industries results were inconclusive. The results reported in his paper, as Koutsoyiannis concludes:

provide evidence against the profit-maximization and sales-maximization hypotheses, and in support of the entry-forestalling hypothesis. Our findings reinforce the results of earlier studies, which suggest that oligopolistic firms, recognizing the long-run costs for short-run greed, produce over the inelastic part of their demand curve in order to avoid the dangers of new entry and/or government intervention. (1984: 540)

Koutsoyiannis' results indirectly provide empirical evidence for the entry-preventing aspect of profit-targeting behaviour. The following sections provide direct empirical tests for such behaviour. But, first, a recent empirical study by Gupta (1988) on the leading role of investments as theorized in the earlier chapters should be mentioned. Gupta attempts to identify the direction of causality between profits and investments as it is hypothesized in the neoclassical, Keynesian and post-Keynesian models. Whereas neoclassical models emphasize causality running from profits to investment, the Keynesian and post-Keynesian models hypothesize the reverse causality. Gupta bases his empirical analysis on the most refined Granger–Sims causality test procedures. However, causality tests, as Gupta acknowledges, should not be construed as proving or disproving a particular economic hypothesis because the tests lack theoretical content. Nevertheless, Gupta's causality tests based on transfer-function models support the hypothesis that the thread of causality is stronger from investment to profits. In addition, he supplements his test results with *ex post* and *ex ante* forecastability of the alternative hypothesis within the transfer-function model framework. He finds that: 'the Keynesian/post-Keynesian hypothesis of causality from investment to profits is definitely superior in terms of forecastability both within and beyond the sample period' (p.19). His empirical findings, that strongly support the thread of causality running from investment to profits, are in the same direction with the results we obtained from the structural model based on the profit-targeting theory.

The Model

To test profit-targeting behaviour, I constructed a price variable based on equation 4.16 of Chapter 4 (see p. 89) to explain the behaviour of the actual prices at the two-digit industry level. The model that I tested is formally expressed as follows:

$$\Delta \ln P_t = \alpha_0 + \alpha_1 \Delta \ln \hat{P}t + u_t \qquad (5.1)$$

where

P_t = actual price
$\hat{P}_t$ = price constructed on the basis of profit-targeting behaviour of equation 4.16 of Chapter 4
u_t = error term

In this equation, the coefficient of the predicted price, α_1, is expected to be unity if firms target their profits as suggested by the model in Chapter 4.

This approach is similar to the one adopted by Coutts, *et al.* (1978) in their test of the 'normal price hypothesis' for manufacturing industries in the UK. According to this view, the firm calculates the level of costs at a normal level of output and sets prices as mark-up on normal costs without reference to temporary variations in demand. To test the normal price hypothesis, the authors normalize labour, material, fuel, indirect taxes and service costs and apply a constant mark-up to normal unit costs. The basic difference between the two approaches is that Coutts *et al.* assume constant mark-up while profit-targeting focuses on the determinants of mark-up.

Coutts *et al.* present the normal price hypothesis as a rationalization of the actual behaviour of industrial firms without presenting a theoretical interpretation of such behaviour. In the brief section they devote to the theory of the firm, they profess to adhere to what they call the behavioural approach where 'firms have an inconsistent set of objectives, or perhaps no well-defined objectives at all'.[1] They find their results to be consistent with that approach rather than a neoclassical or managerial view.

The cost-plus nature of the pricing equation of the profit-targeting model is strongly supported by empirical evidence.[2] In particular the pricing equation of Chapter 4 is completely consistent with Coutts *et al*'s conclusion that 'given costs, final prices decrease with increases in demand' or Houthakker's finding, that the growth of output and price changes are negatively correlated. Semmler's conclusion that cost-plus pricing 'is not limited to concentrated oligopolized industries but seems to be a widespread procedure and can be found in concentrated and non-concentrated industries' (Semmler 1984: 102; see also Sawyer 1983: 97), or Sawyer's conclusion that 'demand may have long-term effects, operating through output, profits and investment' (1983: 93) are supportive of the formulations presented in this study.

Equation 5.1 is tested using annual data in contrast to Coutts *et al*'s use of quarterly data. The year represents the firm's planning period better than the quarter. It is reasonable to suppose that firms have a relatively longer time horizon than a year, but the year is the standard accounting time unit for firms of all types. Furthermore, as Sylos-Labini (1979) notes, the annual data take care of the normalization procedures that Coutts *et al.* go through in using quarterly data.

Industry is the unit of empirical analysis. Aggregate data, such as those on non-financial corporations, do not permit one to analyse industry characteristics such as maturity level, technological dynamics and output growth, which form the core of the present analysis. Disaggregate analysis also enables account to be taken of taxation effects, which are the focus of the financial structure literature in the Modigliani–Miller tradition. Any differences in the financial structures of industries should be explained by factors other than taxation since the taxation effect would be common to all industries.

The industry level seems appropriate compared to the firm level for several reasons:

- Prices are set at the industry level.
- When the price leader sets the price, other firms in the industry will take the price as given. This will lead to a distribution of firms with different IF/I structures. Less efficient firms will borrow to stay competitive. Industry IF/I ratios take into account distribution in each industry and reflect the profitability and competitiveness of the industries relative to other industries.
- An analysis of firms in an industry gives the profitability

of some firms relative to other firms in the industry. What we are interested in is the relative profitability of the industries as reflected in their pricing behaviour and IF/I ratios.

Data

The number of industries included in the econometric testing was determined by the availability of the data, particularly of planned investment data. According to the theoretical argument of Chapter 4, pricing decisions of firms are determined by investment decisions and the costs of inputs. The planned investment data were available at the two-digit SIC level and only for 12 manufacturing industries. These data were published in the February 1985 issue of the *Survey of Current Business*.

The second constraint of the data was the price variable. Price data are collected by the US Labor Bureau on a commodity basis. This implied the need for matching the commodity classification of the Labor Bureau data with the SIC industry classification. This was possible for ten industries.

The data on profit and depreciation are reported at the company level. The US Bureau of Economic Analysis collects the financial data at the company level by assigning the activities of companies to their major field of industry. This implies that as the disaggregation level increases, the reliability of data for the pricing hypothesis declines. The multi-industry companies are assigned to their major activity industries. This leads to an increasing distortion of the industry data as the disaggregation level increases. At a highly aggregated level, such as total manufacturing, this problem is substantially eliminated since all the activities of the companies are accounted for under one or another set of industry data at the total manufacturing level of aggregation. The results of the disaggregated industry level are, then, subject to data limitations. This is clear from the comparisons of the results at the total manufacturing and two-digit industry levels. The latter results are weak relative to the former in terms of R^2 and the size of the coefficients.

Estimation of the Model

In order to test the profit-targeting behaviour, a price variable was constructed on the basis of the price equation in Chapter 4. $\hat{P}_t$ was constructed as follows:

$$\hat{P}_t = a_1 W_t + a_2 M_t + a_3 \frac{\pi_t}{Q_e} \qquad (5.2)$$

where

$\hat{P}_t$ = the price variable constructed on the basis of profit-targeting behaviour

W_t = index of compensation of employees per unit of output taken from *Survey of Current Business*

M_t = index of material costs per unit of output were calculated from the *Annual Survey of Manufacturers*

π_t = profit targets. According to the theoretical arguments of Chapter 4 profit targets are determined by investment decisions. For this reason the planned investment data from the February 1985 issue of the *Survey of Current Business* were used. That is, π = planned investment

Q_e = the expected output variable is a four-year moving average calculated from the production index for manufacturing taken from the *Economic Report of the President*, 1983

a_i = weights used in adding the above indices to arrive at a price index

The sum of $a_1 + a_2 + a_3 = 1$. Weights were calculated from shares of L, M and π in the value of output. These weights were 0.27 for labour, 0.54 for material inputs and 0.19 for profits between 1961–81 and 0.24 for labour, 0.57 for material inputs and 0.19 for profits between 1974–81 for total manufacturing.

Estimation at the Total Manufacturing Level

Since the data at the two-digit level are not as accurate as at the total manufacturing level, the results are reported separately. Additional tests were undertaken at the total manufacturing industry level.

If firms are targeting their profits as suggested by our analysis, then we should expect to find the equation fitting closely with α_1, the coefficient on $\ln \hat{P}_t$, equal to unity. The results for total manufacturing were as follows:

$$\Delta \ln \mathrm{P}_t = 0.00795 + 0.98679 \, \Delta \ln \hat{P}_t \qquad R^2 = 0.9397$$
$$\phantom{\Delta \ln \mathrm{P}_t =} (1.985) \quad\;\; (15.784)$$

t-ratios are in parentheses.

To correct for serial correlation, the second order error process is used. The coefficient of the $\Delta \ln \hat{P}_t$ is significant at the level 0.0001. The results are in conformity with the profit-targeting theory as the coefficient of the constructed price variable is almost equal to unity. Profit-targeting behaviour is very strongly supported at the total manufacturing level.

These results compare favourably against those of Coutts *et al.* who assumed constant mark-up at its 1963 level. They explain only 50 per cent of the variation in prices while the results reported above explain 94 per cent. Also Coutts *et al.*'s coefficients are around 0.6, which are considerably less than 1.

To further test the robustness of the above results, the following equation was tested:

$$\Delta \ln P_t = b_o + b_1 \, \Delta \ln W_t + b_2 \, \Delta \ln M_t + b_3 \, \Delta \ln \pi_t / Q_e$$

If the hypothesis suggested is correct, it is expected that $b_1 + b_2 + b_3 = 1$. The results are:

$$\ln P_t = 0.009 + 0.242 \, 1_n W_t + 0.659 \, 1_n M_t + 0.092 \, 1 n \pi_t / Q_e$$
$$ (2.50) \quad\;\; (1.93) \qquad\quad (7.53) \qquad\qquad (2.56)$$

where

$$b_1 + b_2 + b_3 = 0.993 \qquad R^2 = 0.97$$

While the coefficient of W_t is significant at the 0.07 level, the coefficients of M_t and π_t / Q_e are significant at the 0.0001 and

0.01 levels respectively.

This equation also permits one to test for possible lags between costs and prices. However, the inclusion of several lagged variables did not improve the R^2. In addition, all the coefficients turned out to be insignificant except current M_t. These results support the construction of equation 5.2 (see p.103). As Sylos-Labini (1979) notes, lags are important when quarterly data are used and annual data adjust for quarterly lags. Theoretically, there is no reason for firms' decision-makers to base their pricing decisions on historical rather than replacement costs. The contractual nature of labour and input costs permits firms to calculate replacement costs accurately. Empirical tests clearly support the hypothesis that firms base their decisions on replacement costs.

In order to test whether the planned investment decisions in period t determine the profits at period t as argued in Chapter 4, current profits are regressed on current planned investment decisions:

$$\pi_t = 0.9 \text{ investment decisions}_t \qquad R^2 = 0.97$$
$$(27.364)$$

As expected, the coefficient of the investment decision is significant at the 0.0001 level. The regression of profits on lagged investment decisions, investments and lagged profit variables did not produce significant coefficients.

A final check whether investment decisions in period t determine investment expenditures in period $t+1$ through liquidity constraints, as indicated by profits in period t, was made. The results are as follows:

$$I_{t+1} = 0.83 \text{ Investment decisions}_t + 0.21\,\pi_t \qquad R^2 = 0.997$$
$$(17.73) \qquad\qquad\qquad (3.99)$$

The coefficient of the investment decision variable is significant at the 0.0001 level while that of the profit variable is significant at 0.0006. That is, planned investment decisions in period t determine profits in period t through firms' pricing decisions. Profits earned in period t are being used to finance investment expenditures in period $t+1$. While investment decisions in period t are highly influential in determining the investment expenditures in period $t+1$, firms take into account information and liquidity provided by the profits realized in period t when undertaking investments in period $t+1$.

Estimations at the Two-Digit Industry Level

The statistical results at the two-digit industry level are reported in Table 5.1. The coefficients of the constructed price variable are highly significant at the 0.0001 level for all industries. If there were no measurement errors and the specification of the constructed price variable was correct, we should expect the equation fitting closely with α_1, the coefficient on the $\Delta ln \, \hat{P}_t$ equal to unity. The range of α_1 changes from 0.60 for the motor vehicles industry to 1.17 for the food industry. The coefficients for the six of the industries lie between 0.71 and 0.96, providing remarkably good support for the model.

Errors in the data and the specification of the constructed price variable will have biased the coefficients downward. The errors arise from the way the data are collected, where the company-level data include cross-industry data. This distorts the data by assigning the company to its major field of industry for the multi-industry companies. This is clear from the comparison of the results at the two-digit industry and total manufacturing levels. At the total manufacturing level, the coefficient of the constructed price level is almost one, with very high explanatory power of the price equation as we would expect from the model. At the two-digit industry level, the coefficients are less than unity with relatively lower R^2s. This makes a plausible argument for the downward bias in the coefficients due to the measurement errors in the data.

A second possible source of measurement error in the data may arise from the construction of the predicted price variable. For example, in the construction of the price variable, an output variable adjusted by the four-year moving average capacity utilization is used. This was based on the belief that firms, while adjusting their expectations according to what happened in the recent past, have a forward-looking perspective. Four-year moving averages also take into account firms' sensitivity to business cycles. This method has produced very good results for the total manufacturing level and might not have worked as well for two-digit industries. One reason is that at the aggregate level, there is a filtering of data which makes the estimation process more robust.

A third possible econometric problem may arise from the specification of the model. In this regard, import prices need

Table 5.1   *Regressions of actual on constructed prices (annually, ten manufacturing industries for the 1961–81 period)*

	α_0	α_1	R^2	Error process
Electrical machinery	0.02 (3.49)	0.61 (6.86)	0.71	OLS
Machinery	0.02 (2.29)	0.72 (4.62)	0.57	AR2
Chemicals	0.02 (1.64)	0.96 (7.78)	0.79	AR2
Textiles	0.01 (0.82)	0.80 (3.12)	0.38	AR2
Fabricated metals	0.02 (1.43)	0.64 (3.85)	0.42	OLS
Paper	0.01 (1.28)	0.78 (6.45)	0.72	AR2
Primary metals	0.02 (2.44)	0.79 (9.19)	0.84	AR2
Food	0.00	1.17 (11.62)	0.89	AR2
Petroleum	0.02 (3.00)	0.71 (18.3)	0.95	OLS
Motor vehicles	0.01 (1.52)	0.60 (4.43)	0.55	AR2

Note: The numbers in parentheses are t-statistics.

to be included in the model to the extent that they affect the pricing behaviour of the domestic industries. Import competition has increased significantly for some individual industries since the early 1970s while affecting the total manufacturing industry to a lesser extent in the same period. This implies that some domestic industries were constrained in their price setting behaviour as the import competition increased. This requires a modification of the model as to take into account the import prices:

$$\Delta ln\, P_t = \alpha_o + \alpha_1\, \Delta ln\, \hat{P}_t + \alpha_2\, \Delta ln\, P_m + u_t$$

where

P_m = import prices

Inclusion of import prices in the model may improve the industry results to the extent that import competition is important in the price-setting behaviour of the industry. Increasing protectionism has the impact of restraining the impact of import competition for the price-setting behaviour of the industry. However, import price-series corresponding to the two-digit SIC industry level for the period 1958–81 were unavailable.

In conclusion, given the data constraints, the two-digit industry regression results show the success and significance of the constructed price variable in explaining the behaviour of actual price movements. Profit-targeting behaviour is strongly supported by empirical evidence.

ECONOMETRIC EVIDENCE ON THE DETERMINANTS OF INTERNAL FINANCING RATIOS

As seen from Table 1.1 in Chapter 1, internal financing ratios differ across industries. They ranged from 0.92 for the electronic machinery industry to 1.29 for the primary and fabricated metals industries with an average of 1.16 for the total manu-

facturing industries in the period 1954–68. In the period 1969–
82, the average declined to 0.99, while the range varied from
0.50 for other transportation industries to 1.42 for the fabricated metals industry. The lower rates in the most recent
period reflect the impact of increasing import competition on
the price-setting ability of US domestic industry. The importance of the differences in internal financing ratios across
industries is that they may reflect the structural differences
within and across industries. To the extent that such differences as technology, capital intensity, maturity and import
competition explain the differences in internal financing
ratios, they will be supporting the development of the modelling of the relationship between the real and financial sectors
presented in Chapter 4. This is important because there is no
study that analyses the inter-industry differences in internal
financing ratios.

In conventional economic theory, inter-industry comparisons are usually made in terms of profit margins. However, it
is difficult to interpret price-cost margin type measures in a
dynamic context. This study suggests the use of IF/I ratios as
the measure of profitability. The advantage of the IF/I ratio is
that it provides an approximate dynamic profitability measure
as compared to the static measures of profitability such as the
Lerner Index of price-cost margins, and others cited in Scherer
(1980, Chapter 9). If the intensity of competition is high in the
industry, price-cost margins may be high not due to the lack of
competition in a static sense but due to the excess of competition in a dynamic sense. For example, high price-cost
margins in the computer industry may translate into low IF/I
ratios, indicating that the firms in the computer industry
invest at high rates to stay competitive in the following periods. In contrast, the low price-cost margins in the textiles
industry may translate into high IF/I ratios as in Table 1.1. If
that is the case, then the prices charged by the textile industry
are not justified by their competitive needs, and the protectionism provided to the textile industry for more than 30 years
might have resulted in the protection of profits in this industry
at the expense of other industries.

The IF/I ratio may be applied as a measure of profitability both at the industry and firm levels. However the interpretation of the ratio at the industry level will differ from its usage at the firm level. At the former level, the ratio should be evaluated according to whether it is less than one or not, rather than assuming a continuous distribution of industries with different IF/I ratios. For example, the size of the IF/I ratio being greater than one can be interpreted as the profitability of the industry being high relative to the survival requirements in the industry as indicated by the relative size of investment efforts of firms in the industry. It can be argued that due to the existence of entry barriers or government intervention, such as protectionism, firms in the industry are enjoying excess profits. IF/I ratios less than one may imply the existence of competitive conditions in the industry. In this case again it is difficult to rank industries with IF/I ratios less than one because structural factors may account for the differences. For example, IF/I ratios need to be adjusted for the growth rates of the industries. In high-growth industries, we may observe lower IF/I ratios relative to low-growth industries.

The target IF/I ratio of one is important because an increase in the intensity of competition will be reflected in higher observed $R\&D/I$ ratios in the industry. As shown in Chapter 4, this increases the possibilities of undertaking investment projects with rates of return less than the cost of borrowing. The risky nature of technological competition asks for reliable sources of funds. Firms will tend to generate larger amounts of internal funds, pushing the IF/I ratio up towards one. That is, in industries with IF/I ratios less than one, as the intensity of competition increases, as reflected in higher $R\&D/I$ ratios, IF/I ratios tend to increase because competition induces technological changes which are mostly financed out of internal funds. For industries with IF/I ratios higher than one, since internal funds are already high relative to investment expenditures, the above relationship between the intensity of competition and the IF/I ratio weakens. An increase in the intensity of competition will push IF/I ratios downwards towards one as entry barriers and/or government intervention, which permitted the IF/I ratios to be higher than one to begin with, dissolve.

At the firm level, the IF/I ratios need to be interpreted differently. Since the prices are set at the average efficiency level in the industry, there will be a distribution of firms with different IF/I ratios around the industry average. Firms having IF/I ratios greater than the industry average will be the most competitive firms in the industry. The less efficient firms will be resorting to external funds to stay competitive, reflected in IF/I ratios less than the industry average. This makes the IF/I ratio the appropriate measure of dynamic profitability at both the firm and industry levels.

At the industry level, the IF/I ratio by itself may not provide an absolute measure of profitability unless the dividend–payout ratio is taken into account. If dividend–payout ratios vary across industries, it may become difficult to interpret the differences in the IF/I ratios. For the industries with IF/I ratios above one, it may still be argued that these industries generate more funds than they need in order to stay competitive; in other words, they are profitable relative to industries with IF/I ratios less than one.

A measure that takes into account the dividend–payout ratio might be constructed by adding dividends to the IF/I ratio. That is, $IF + D/I + D$. In this measure, the division of the internal funds into dividend and investment expenditures becomes unimportant. The relevant consideration is whether the firm is able to generate funds to finance its expenditures. The necessary expenditures are considered to be investment and dividend payments. Liquidity needs in the short run are not considered a necessary expenditure because they arise due to the time pattern of the firm's receipts and expenditures, which can be overcome by short-term borrowing or the acquisition and disposal of financial assets.

It should be emphasized again that by financial structure the ratio of external to internal financing of the firms is meant. Emphasis on external versus internal funds is different from the Modigliani–Miller tradition of the finance literature, which concentrates on the mix of debt, especially on the debt-equity relationship even though new stock issues of non-financial corporations have formed only 2 per cent of their total sources of funds in the post-World War II period in the USA (see Taggart 1984, Table 2). The basic reason for the Modigliani–Miller tradition's failure to emphasize the importance of internal funds lies in the separation of firm's real decisions from financing decisions. Modigliani–Miller does not analyse the pricing behaviour of firms in the product market or try to establish its relation to the financing behaviour of the firms as it is done in this study.

Another indicator that is used by many authors when firms' borrowing trends are discussed is the ratio of internal funds to total sources of funds. Most of these authors tend to use the ratio as evidence to support the profit-squeeze argument (for example, Pollin 1983). However, a declining trend in the ratio may not imply a profit squeeze, as a declining trend in the IF/I ratio would imply. In the 1970s, the internal funds–total sources of funds ratio was declining mainly because firms were borrowing to acquire financial assets. This had the effect of increasing the denominator. It was not the case that firms' profits were squeezed and they could not finance their investment expenditures.

The Model

The importance of the structural variables specified in Chapter 4 can be tested using the following model:

$$IF/I = \beta_0 + \beta_1 K/Y + \beta_2 \dot{Q} + \beta_3 M + \beta_4 R\&D/I \qquad (5.3)$$

where

K/Y = capital–output ratio
$\dot{Q}$ = the growth rate of the output
M = import penetration ratio – the ratio of imports to domestic sales plus imports
$R\&D/I$ = ratio of $R\&D$ expenditures to investment expenditures as an indicator of the technological dynamics and the intensity of competition in the industry.

The impact of the capital–output ratio on the internal

funds–investment ratio depends on the nature of the constraints on industry behaviour and the availability of capital. From the definition of profitability, $\pi/Y = \pi/K.K/Y$, if profitability or price is given, an increase in the K/Y ratio means a decline in the rate of return. If the rate of return in the industry is already high, a decline in the rate of profit may not affect the borrowing abilities of firms. In this case, the relationship between the capital–output ratio and the IF/I ratio is negative since firms are able to finance their capital expenditures through borrowing. Given profitability, if an increase in the K/Y ratio reduces the rate of return to the level that affects the borrowing ability, the tendency of the increased K/Y ratio will be to increase the IF/I ratio through a decline in the dividend-payout ratio or disposing of financial assets. If profitability is changing while the K/Y ratio is increasing, the impact of the K/Y ratio will depend on the relative changes in profitability and the K/Y ratio within the context of the two cases discussed earlier.

The assumption that price is given may reflect the constraint on the price-setting behaviour of firms due to import competition. Increasing import competition may induce domestic industries to modernize or automate, which will increase the K/Y ratio. That is, we may expect a close relationship between import penetration and the K/Y ratios whenever import competition puts pressure on domestic firms to respond by improving their competitiveness rather than resorting to protectionist lobbying.

Import competition constrains the domestic firms' ability to set prices. This has a negative impact on their profit margin and thus on the IF/I ratio as long as it is not counteracted by protectionist measures. The import competition variable is measured by the import penetration ratio, which is defined as the ratio of imports to domestic sales plus imports. The obvious weakness of this ratio is that in the presence of protectionism, either in the form of import quotas or voluntary export restrictions, it may not reflect adequately the impact of competitive pressures from abroad. One may argue that the presence of protectionism may eliminate such competitive pressures anyway. We may find situations in which a slowly increasing import penetration ratio is accompanied by increasing profitability due to the nature of the quota system. The response of the domestic auto industry in the USA to voluntary export restrictions in the 1980s is an example of such a situation. The Japanese auto exporters, knowing that they cannot increase their auto exports beyond the limits of the voluntary export restrictions, followed the price lead of domestic auto producers.

The growth rate of output shifts both the profitability and the vulnerability curves. As the growth rate of output increases, the *IF/I* ratio may tend to decline if the rate of change in investment exceeds the rate of growth in internal funds. This is the case when firms do not push up the prices to the full extent so as not to put brakes on the growth rate of output; and the availability of capital due to growth prospects may lessen their need for internal funds. In this case, the growth rate of output and the *IF/I* ratio are inversely related.

The technological dynamics of the industry are represented by the ratio of *R&D* expenditures to investment expenditures. Rather than using the conventional measure of the *R&D*/sales ratio, the *R&D*/investment ratio is preferred. This is because

$$\frac{R\&D}{\text{sales}} = \frac{R\&D}{I} \star \frac{I}{\text{sales}}$$

which implies that the *R&D*/sales ratio is not an accurate measure of the technological dynamics of the industry. Even if the *R&D/I* ratio is low, the *R&D*/sales ratio could be high if the *I*/sales ratio is high. The *I*/sales ratio is related to the incremental capital to sales rather than to technological dynamics. It might be high because in a technologically stable industry, firms are investing to meet increasing demand. The *R&D/I* ratio takes into account the technological dynamics of the industry more accurately. In technologically dynamic industries where the *R&D/I* ratio is high, we may expect more reliance on internal funds since technological innovation involves relatively riskier investments. That is, the *R&D/I* ratio and the *IF/I* ratio are positively correlated.

Data

The number of the industries was limited to 12 due to the availability of investment expenditure data. Time-series data for most of the variables have been available since 1958.

Estimation of the Model

Time-series analyses were run for the period 1958–81. The sample of industries was too small for meaningful cross-section regression results. To overcome the sample size limitations, cross-section time-series analyses were run.

It has not been possible to test the general model with all the variables included for the time-series analysis of each industry. The multi-collinearity problem showed up seriously in some of the industry regressions.[3] The high correlation between the industry variables was an expected result of industry response to developments in the economy. But the response of each industry has been different depending on structural characteristics. Technologically stable industries may emphasize modernization (and maybe an increase in the K/Y ratio) in the face of import competition, whereas technologically dynamic industries may try to promote their technological lead by increasing $R\&D$ expenditures. This implies a very high correlation between import competition and $R\&D$ expenditures. For example, in technologically stable industries, such as fabricated and primary metals, firms, knowing that the product cycles of new innovation are too short to make $R\&D$ expenditures on new products profitable, responded by reducing their new product expenditures.

The presence of protectionist policies also influences the behaviour of both domestic and foreign firms. In the motor vehicles industry in the USA, for example, domestic firms argued for restrictions on the market share of foreign firms. Voluntary export restraints enabled domestic auto firms to continue to set prices without being challenged by foreign firms. For these reasons, in the time-series regression for each industry appropriate changes were made to take into account the multi-collinearity problem caused by the response of the industry under consideration. For each industry, the best performing equations are reported. The method used for correction of serial correlation is also indicated.

Fabricated Metals

In the fabricated metal industry, the growth rate was 3.3 per cent per year for the 1958–81 period. However, increasing import competition has led to an increase in the capital–output ratio but a decline in *R&D* spending as revealed by high correlation ratios between the import share and K/Y and the import share and $R&D/I$ variables. For this reason the model for the fabricated metals industry was estimated with only output and import-competition variables. The estimation with K/Y, M and the $R&D/I$ variables included led to high standard errors for the coefficients of these variables indicating multi-collinearity already predicted by high correlations between these variables.

$$IF/I = 1.31 + 0.039M - 1.105Q$$
$$(26.1)\quad(2.1)\quad(-3.01)$$
$$R^2 = 0.42\quad\text{OLS}$$

The import penetration is significant at the 5 per cent level and the growth rate of output is significant at a level lower than 1 per cent.

Primary Metals

In the primary metals industry, the growth rate for the period of 1958–81 was 2.4 per cent per year. The dramatic increase in import competition led to a sudden increase in the capital–output ratio. A decline in *R&D* spending in the late 1960s was reversed in the 1970s due to diversification of the companies into new fields.

The high correlation between import share and the capital–output ratio led to a choice of a model with only the capital–output ratio included.

$$IF/I = 1.25 - 0.97\,Q + 0.05\,R\&D/I - 0.29\,KY$$
$$\ (9.2)\quad (-4.0)\qquad (5.6)\qquad\ (-6.5)$$
$$R^2 = 0.79 \qquad AR1$$

All the coefficients are highly significant at the 0.0001 level. While the output growth and capital–output variables have negative signs, the sign of the coefficient of the $R\&D/I$ variable is positive. The negative sign of the capital–output ratio can be explained by the inability of firms to raise internal funds for modernization in the face of increasing import competition.

Non-electrical Machinery

The growth rate of the non-electrical machinery industry was 5.5 per cent per year in the 1958–81 period. An increase in the import-penetration share is matched by a slight increase in the K/Y ratio.

$$IF/I = 1.97 + 0.08\,M - 1.92\,K/Y - 0.099\,Q + 0.01\,R\&D/I$$
$$\ (4.8)\quad (2.05)\quad\ (-2.83)\quad (-2.05)\qquad (4.28)$$
$$R^2\ = 0.73 \qquad AR1$$

While output and import-competition variables are significant at the 5 per cent level, the $R\&D/I$ and K/Y variables are significant at the 1 per cent level. The response of firms in non-electrical machinery to increasing import competition indicates that domestic firms have allowed the import penetration ratio to rise rather than reducing prices in the face of increasing import competition. This has enabled them to maintain profitability, permitting easier access to borrowing for modernization purposes. This is clear from the positive import-penetration coefficient associated with a negative coefficient on the K/Y ratio.

Paper

The paper industry grew by 4.2 per cent per year in the 1958–81 period. While the import share and $R\&D/I$ ratios changed little, there was an increase in the K/Y ratio in the industry over the same period.

$$IF/I = 0.2\,M - 1.39\,Q + 0.05\,R\&D/I - 0.5\,K/Y$$
$$\ (2.7)\quad (-2.7)\qquad (2.9)\qquad (-6.7)$$
$$R^2 = 0.67\qquad \text{OLS}$$

All the variables in this equation are highly significant.

Chemical Products

The growth rate for the chemical products in the 1958–81 period was 6.7 per cent a year. While import penetration and capital–output ratios rose, there was a decline in the $R\&D/I$ ratio. Due to a high correlation between the K/Y ratio, the import share variable and the $R\&D/I$ ratio and output growth variable, the preferred equation for the chemical industry is the one with only the $R\&D/I$ and M variables. Equations with other variables had slightly higher R^2s but the variables were not significant.

$$IF/I = 0.57 - 0.06\,M + 0.011\,R\&D/I$$
$$\ (2.8)\quad (-2.2)\qquad (4.3)$$
$$R^2 = 0.84\qquad AR1$$

Motor Vehicles

The growth rate for the motor vehicles industry was 3.9 per cent per year in the 1958–81 period. There has been a dramatic increase in the import-penetration ratio since the late 1960s. There was a decline in the $R\&D/I$ ratio and an increase in the K/Y ratio.

$$IF/I = 1.6 + 0.026\,M - 1.37\,Q + 0.003\,R\&D/I - 0.81\,K/Y$$
$$\ (7.97)\quad (2.69)\quad (-3.85)\qquad (1.013)\qquad (-4.3)$$
$$R^2 = 0.63\qquad AR2$$

All variables other than the $R\&D/I$ ratio are highly significant.

Food

The growth rate for the food industry was 3.2 per cent per year in the 1958–81 period. There was a slight decrease in the $R\&D/$

I ratio but an increase in both K/Y and import share ratios.

$$IF/I = -0.13\ M + 4.04\ Q + 0.15\ R\&D/I + 0.20\ K/Y$$
$$\qquad (-1.8) \qquad (3.3) \qquad\quad (2.9) \qquad\qquad (1.2)$$
$$R^2 = 0.74 \qquad\qquad AR2$$

Only the K/Y ratio is not significant in this equation.

Stone and Clay

The growth rate for the stone and clay industry was 2.6 per cent per year for the 1958–81 period. While the capital–output ratios rose, there was a decline in the $R\&D/I$ ratio. A high correlation between the capital–output ratio and import share called for exclusion of one of these variables. The regression without the K/Y ratio variable has a higher R^2 but the output growth variable becomes insignificant. For this reason the regression with the capital–output ratio included is reported.

$$IF/I = 1.36 - 0.808\ Q + 0.021\ R\&D/I - 0.32\ K/Y$$
$$\qquad (7.9) \quad (2.9) \qquad\quad (2.8) \qquad\qquad (-5.7)$$
$$R^2 = 0.78 \qquad AR2$$

Rubber and Plastics

The growth rate of rubber and plastics in the 1958–81 period was 8.1 per cent per year. The import-penetration ratio rose from 1 per cent in the late 1950s to 5.5 per cent in the early 1980s. While the K/Y ratio doubled during this period, $R\&D/I$ was almost halved. The correlation of the growth rate variable with the remaining variables led the growth rate to become insignificant when run together with another variable. The best equation is the one without the growth rate variable.

$$IF/I = -0.12\ M + 0.016\ R\&D/I + 0.45\ K/Y$$
$$\qquad (-4.52) \qquad\quad (4.61) \qquad\quad (3.48)$$
$$R^2 = 0.80 \qquad AR2$$

Petroleum

The growth rate of output was 2.7 per cent during the period 1958–81. There were slight increases in the import-penetration and capital–output ratios but a decline in the *R&D/I* ratio. The correlation coefficients between the independent variables for the petroleum industry are higher than the correlation coefficients between dependent and independent variables. This has made a meaningful regression analysis difficult for the petroleum industry.

$$IF/I = 0.028\,M + 0.064\,R\&D/I + 0.17\,K/Y$$
$$\quad\quad (1.53) \quad\quad\quad (1.70) \quad\quad\quad (1.74)$$
$$R^2 = 0.39 \quad AR1$$

In this equation, the *R&D/I* and *K/Y* ratios are significant only at the 10 per cent level, constituting the worst result among the industry time-series analysis. This is most probably due to the facts that the petroleum industry is heavily based on raw materials and the oil markets were very turbulent in the 1970s, which lies outside of the focus of the model tested.

Textiles

The textiles industry grew by 3.4 per cent in the 1958–81 period. There was a slight increase in the import-penetration ratio. The *R&D/I* ratio declined where as the *K/Y* ratio increased. High correlations between the growth rate and capital-output ratio and *R&D/I* and import-penetration ratios have reduced the best performing equation to the one with two variables.

$$IF/I = 0.10\,R\&D/I + 0.21\,K/Y$$
$$\quad\quad (4.37) \quad\quad\quad (1.86)$$
$$R^2 = 0.56 \quad AR2$$

The equations with the other two variables also had significant coefficients but with smaller R^2s.

Electrical Machinery

The growth rate for the electrical machinery industry was 6.6 per cent in the 1958–81 period. The import-penetration ratio

Table 5.2   *Summary of the coefficients of time series regressions on internal-financing ratios*

	Q	*M*	*R&D/I*	*K/Y*
Positive and significant	2	4	9	4
Positive and insignificant	0	1	2	1
Negative and significant	6	3	0	5
Negative and insignificant	0	0	0	0

rose from 1.3 per cent in the late 1950s to 12.2 per cent in 1981. During this period the K/Y ratio doubled to 1.34, whereas the $R&D/I$ ratio was more than halved. An almost perfect correlation between the K/Y ratio and the import-penetration variable leaves an equation with three variables.

$$IF/I = 0.57 \, Q + 0.002 \, R&D/I + 0.57 \, K/Y$$
$$\quad\quad (2.1) \quad\quad\quad (4.3) \quad\quad\quad (4.7)$$
$$R^2 = 0.62 \quad\quad AR2$$

A Summary of the Results

The results of the regression for the time-series analyses are summarized so as to evaluate the relative importance of the independent variables. Table 5.2 gives a summary of the coefficients.

The most consistent coefficient of the regressions has been the one on the $R&D/I$ ratio. The $R&D/I$ variable has turned out to be significant in 9 of the 11 industries with a positive sign. This clearly shows the risky nature of technological innovation. As firms have increased $R&D$ expenditures relative to investments, they have done so by increasing the internally financed portion of investment. One implication of this result is that firms' ability to innovate is constrained by the availability of internal funds. To the extent that firms' ability to raise internal funds is restricted by import competition, $R&D$ expenditures will suffer the most. This has been true for all the industries that have experienced an increase in the import-penetration ratio. The policy implication is that the availability of risk capital is important for the ability of firms to undertake technological innovation. This is a crucial factor in the competitiveness of domestic firms on the world markets.

The empirical evidence on the positive and significant effect of the $R\&D/I$ ratio on the IF/I ratio for 9 industries strongly supports the conceptual suggestions of this study. Competition results in technological change rather than being restricted to the pricing decisions of firms as in neoclassical economics. As the intensity of competition increases, as measured by the $R\&D/I$ ratio, the dynamic profitability of firms, as measured by the IF/I ratio, increases. This is in sharp contrast to neoclassical economics, where an increase in competition, as measured by the number of firms existing in the industry, reduces profits of firms in a static sense, measured by profit margins. At the limit of the perfect-competition case, the profit margins are zero! This results from the static nature and price focus of the neoclassical approach. In the dynamic approach developed in this study, as competition increases a higher rate of technological change is induced with an increasing degree of uncertainty. Firms rely on internal funds to undertake investments that will enable their survival, implying the need for a higher profitability (IF/I) in the dynamic sense.

The output growth-rate variable has a negative sign for six industries (fabricated metals, primary metals, non-electrical machinery, paper, motor vehicles, and stone–clay) and a positive sign for two industries (food and electrical machinery).

The import-penetration ratio has a positive coefficient for five industries (fabricated metals, non-electrical machinery, paper, motor vehicles and petroleum) and negative for three industries (chemical, food and rubber). This indicates the importance of the interaction between domestic firms and foreign firms in determining the domestic firms' behaviour. In some industries, import competition has been challenged by non-price measures such as voluntary export restraints which have helped to maintain the profit margins for the domestic firms. This has led to a positive sign on the import-penetration ratio. In the industries where price competition has been prevalent, the import-competition variable has a negative sign, indicating the inability of domestic firms to raise internal funds to finance their expenditures in the face of import competition.

The sign of the coefficients on the K/Y ratio reveals some interesting factors at work. For five industries it is positive (electrical, textiles, petroleum, rubber and food); for the other five industries it is negative (primary metal, stone–clay, motor vehicles, paper, non-electrical machinery). For all the industries, there has been an increase in the K/Y ratio over the period, resulting in part from the domestic industries' attempt to modernize in order to maintain the competitiveness against imports. The regression results give an idea about how the modernization efforts of the domestic industries were financed and why they were financed as they were. From the discussion in Chapter 4, we would expect that, given the profitability, an increase in the K/Y ratio would reduce the rate of return on capital. This will have a tendency to limit access to financial markets. Thus, we would expect that, as the price-setting power (or profitability) of firms is reduced, their modernization efforts would be financed through internal funds rather than borrowing. That is, there would be a positive relationship between the K/Y ratio and IF/I ratio when the profitability is impaired due to import competition. As the regression results for the rubber–plastics and food industries show, when the import-penetration ratio coefficient is negative, the coefficient on the K/Y ratio is positive; on the other hand, when the coefficient of the import-penetration ratio is positive, indicating the relative absence of price pressure on domestic industries as in motor vehicles, paper and non-electrical machinery industries, the coefficient on the K/Y ratio is negative. This implies that firms' access to financial markets was not impaired by import competition, and that firms financed their modernization efforts through financial markets. Only in the petroleum industry is there a positive coefficient for the import-penetration ratio accompanied by a positive coefficient on the K/Y ratio. This is not difficult to explain given that the IF/I ratio in the industry increased over the period. The availability of internal funds reduced the need for external

financing. For the remaining industries, the import-penetration ratio was excluded from the regressions due to multi-
collinearity. For two of these industries (electrical machinery
and textiles), the coefficients on the K/Y ratio were positive,
and for stone–clay and primary-metals industries they were
negative.

A final comment on the time-series regression equations
concerns the decline in the explanatory power of the model for
industries with IF/I ratios above one. For the fabricated
metals, textiles, and petroleum industries where the IF/I ratios
higher than one persisted over the period, the R^2s were around
0.40. Protectionist tendencies in the textiles industry and oil-
price increases in the 1970s in the petroleum industry weakened the relationship between the IF/I ratio and the structural
characteristics of the industries. In general, one would expect
the weakening of the relationship whenever the pricing behaviour of the industry is determined by non-structural variables.
In cases of declining industries with import protectionism,
firms set prices to collect what can be called 'rents' without
inducing entry. In these industries, the IF/I ratios over one will
persist as long as firms are isolated from competition.

Cross-Section Time-Series Estimations

The small size of the sample (12 industries) limits the use of the
cross-section regression analysis in determining the importance of the several variables suggested. It is not possible to
obtain meaningful results for a small sample run with four
independent variables. To overcome the limitations of the
sample size, the cross-section and time-series data have been
combined using the DaSilva method. This estimates the
regression parameters with a two-step generalized least-
squares type estimator or the generalized least squares with
the unknown covariance matrix replaced by a suitable esti-
mater. The results are as follows:

$$IF/I = 1.26 - 0.05\ M - 0.07\ K/Y + 0.004\ R\&D/I - 0.41\ Q$$
$$\quad\quad (31.4)\quad (-36.2)\quad (-9.9)\quad\quad (27.4)\quad\quad (-36.9)$$

All the variables are highly significant. Results from the pooling of the cross-section and time-series regression data are similar to the time-series results, reaffirming the importance of the variables used. In particular, the consistent positive sign and significance of the $R\&D/I$ ratio gives further empirical evidence for using this ratio as a measure of competitive behaviour.

NOTES

1. Coutts *et al.* (1978: 96–9).
2. See Sawyer (1983), Semmler (1984a) for a survey of the econometric research. See Coutts *et al.* (1978), Houthakker (1979), Koutsoyiannis (1984) and Sawyer (1983) for econometric research at the industry level.
3. For detection of multi-collinearity and solutions to the multi-collinearity problem see Pindyck and Rubinfield (1981).

APPENDIX 5.1: DATA SOURCES

Price = Producer Price Index, *Business Statistics* (1982) and *Handbook of Labor Statistics*, US Department of Labor

Production Index = *Business Statistics* (1982), US Department of Commerce

Capacity Utilization Index = *McGraw Hill Annual Surveys, Business Plans for New Plants and Equipment*, several years

Profits = *National Income and Product Accounts* (1986), US Department of Commerce

Capital Consumption Allowances = *National Income and Product Accounts* (1986)

Compensation of Employees = *National Income and Product Accounts* (1986)

Planned Investment = *Survey of Current Business*, February 1985

Investment = *Survey of Current Business*, February 1985

Gross Fixed Capital Stock = *Survey of Current Business*, July 1985

Gross National Product by Industry = *National Income and Product Accounts* (1986)

Sales = *Business Statistics* (1982)

Imports = *US Commodity Exports and Imports as Related to Output*, several years

R&D Expenditure = *Research and Development in Industry*, National Science Foundation, several years

Material Costs = *Annual Survey of Manufacturers*, several years

Net Interest Payments = *Corporation Income Tax Returns*, Internal Revenue Service, several years

Weights in matching the commodity classification with the industry classification = *Supplement to the Producer Price Index*, US Department of Labor

6. Financial Systems and Firm Behaviour: Comparative and International Perspectives

In earlier chapters, the crucial importance of the financial system of the economy for determining the availability and conditions of loanable funds has been emphasized. Of particular interest was how the availability and conditions of loanable funds affect firm behaviour through competition, given the institutional assumption of the existence of a securities-based financial system.

Firm behaviour, in the context of earlier chapters, refers to the pricing, investment and financial-structure decisions of firms. Table 1.2 (Chapter 1) showed that the financial structures of firms differ from one country to another. This chapter attempts to explain these differences. The interaction between the real and financial sectors is examined from comparative and international perspectives. The experience of the US, Japanese and West German financial systems is briefly reviewed to show that national differences in the institutional structures of these countries were influential in determining the nature of relationships between the real and financial sectors. The argument is that the financial systems of these three successful countries in the post-World War II period were distinctively different. Diversity in firm behaviour in terms of technological dynamics and financing patterns might have resulted from the inherent biases of the financial systems present in these countries. The comparative analysis of the countries is, then, extended to statistical analyses in the international context.

The uniqueness of financial systems results from the historical and institutional background of each country. Firms find themselves in a system they have little power to change, and adapt their behaviour to the availability and conditions of funds on the financial markets. This is not to say that financial systems do not change, but rather that it requires more than the action of a single firm.

The current structure of the financial systems of Japan and West Germany can be traced back to the nineteenth century. Both countries, as late industrializers, needed an infusion of large-scale capital through financial intermediaries that would undertake the risk of industrialization. In Germany, the universal banks were established to accomplish this task. They not only provided the much-needed capital for the industry but, as Gerschenkron (1962) emphasizes, also substituted for entrepreneurial deficiencies.[1] The 1850s witnessed a surge of growth in the heavy capital-goods industries which was essential to German industrialization. The universal banks were actively involved with their own funds in the promotion of the newly emerging branches of industry. They retained a share in the new enterprises so as to exercise supervision over management. The banks expected the funds they had advanced to the enterprises to be repaid from the issue of stocks and bonds once the enterprise was sufficiently well established. The close relationship between banks and firms in Germany today thus has its origins in the beginnings of German industrialization in the nineteenth century.

A similar function was served by the government in Japan, also in the late nineteenth century. During this period, a variety of semi-governmental institutions was established to finance several sectors of the economy. In the 1930s, the Japanese financial system became more centralized, in part because of the growth of the *zaibatsu* (financial groups) and in part through even greater government involvement in financial activities than had existed previously.

Unsuccessful attempts were made by the Allied forces to break down the pre-war financial systems after World War II. As development accelerated in both Germany and Japan in the 1950s, the prewar financial systems reasserted themselves. It was not until the 1970s that the pressures of accumulating fiscal deficits and current-account swings forced Japan to make institutional changes and to deregulate its financial markets.[2]

A typology of the financial markets is developed in this chapter and the inherent biases of each financial system, in terms of financial intermediary–firm relationships, are examined. The US, Japanese and West German financial systems are placed within that typology. A brief description of the financial system in each country is presented, then the bank–industry relations are analysed as qualitative evidence of the hypothesis that each financial system has its own inherent biases. Quantitative support for the argument that the availability of funds to new entrants in each financial system differs is attempted: the concentration ratios across countries are presented – these may indicate the difficulty of entry; the *R&D*/investment ratios are presented so as to argue that a higher ratio of *R&D* to investment implies higher risk-taking behaviour on the part of the firm and the financial system; and the amount of venture capital in each country is shown to indicate the relative availability of risk capital. Hypotheses on the importance of financial systems in influencing the technological dynamics and financing patterns across countries are tested statistically using international data from OECD sources.

TYPES OF FINANCIAL SYSTEMS

The basic function common to all financial systems is to transform the savings of surplus units into the investments undertaken by deficit units in the economy. What distinguishes financial systems from one another is the way in which they do this. The institutional structure of the financial system becomes central because the modes of financial intermediation depend on the institutional arrangements. The distinction between financial systems can be made on the basis of the predominance of a particular mode of external financing by firms. There are two modes of financing: *direct*, and *indirect*. Direct financing takes place when firms raise funds from capital markets; indirect financing is the case when firms meet their financing needs through loans from credit institutions. We can define the financial system on the basis of the relative importance of its institutions: *a securities-based financial system* is one in which capital markets are relatively more important as a source of financing of firms, and a credit-based financial system is one in which indirect financing through loans predominates the financial intermediation process.

In securities-based financial systems, firms raise funds directly from the saving units in the economy independent of the influence of financial intermediaries. The role of those intermediaries is to facilitate the firms' access to the surplus of saving units and, as such, the financial intermediaries are secondary to the existence of the capital markets in financing firms' needs.

Firms raise funds on the capital markets through the issue of bonds and stocks. Other assets sold on the capital markets include mortgages and government bonds. There are two submarkets that essentially comprise what are called capital markets: the primary capital markets are where new issues of securities are sold; the secondary capital markets are where securities already issued are traded. While the primary capital markets signify the creation of new investment funds, the secondary markets permit investors to dispose of their initial investments without being tied up for the whole maturity period of the security. Most buying and selling of securities takes place in the secondary capital markets. The crucial importance of the secondary markets is that they establish a price for the existing financial assets, thus setting the terms on which additional funds can be raised.

The development level of the secondary markets in terms of the number of buyers, sellers and institutions largely determines the ability of capital markets to raise new funds. Large secondary markets imply that any seller is likely to find a buyer, thus reducing the risk of undertaking investment. The large size of the market also tends to dampen price fluctuations that may arise from the transactions of large institutional investors, including government buying and selling of bonds.

Indirect financing takes place when firms borrow from financial intermediaries that draw their funds from deposits, as in the case of banks, or from the bond side of capital markets, as in the specialized lending institutions. Banks are involved in the financing decision actively and actually determine the allocation of funds between firms. In credit-based systems, the financial intermediaries, especially banks, have a primary role in the financing process. This arises from their ability to transform small-size deposits into large investable funds that are a multiple of the deposits. In allocating investable funds, the basic issue is the recovery of funds which will eventually be claimed back by depositors. This forces banks to be actively involved in the lending process in order to secure the soundness of their loans. The established practice of requiring collateral for loan eligibility typically excludes non-established firms from ready access to loanable funds.

The distinction between securities-based and credit-based financial systems arises from the different nature of intermediation in each system. These differences are as follows:

- *The nature of financial intermediation*   Banks' financial intermediation is composed of two integrated activities: borrowing from depositors and lending to firms. Banks' ability to lend is limited by the size of its deposits. This leads banks to compete with each other in attracting deposits. However, a bank's success in attracting deposits may not have any relation to its lending activities as long as the bank's assets are secure. That is, depositors are not interested in the bank's lending activities as long as they are assured of getting their deposits back. Consequently, discretion over lending is solely in the hands of banks in credit-based financial systems which in turn enforces the bank-borrower relationship.

  In securities-based systems, the lender (the investor) invests directly in the securities of firms. The financial intermediaries' function is to facilitate this process; their success depends on the number of opportunities they present to investors. The relationship between the firms and the financial intermediaries is limited since the ultimate choice of investment is determined by the investor.

- *Assumption of risk by financial intermediaries* In credit-based systems, banks assume the responsibility of lending. There are two types of risk: the soundness of bank loans, which would be required for any type of lending and a specific bank-risk. Banks' liabilities are composed of deposits that are mostly of a short-term nature while their loans are of a long-term nature. In the process of striving to adjust the term structure of their assets to that of their liabilities, banks tend to exercise control over their lending to assure the soundness of their business activities.

  In securities-based systems, the risk of lending is assumed by the investor. Financial intermediaries provide investors with a portfolio of securities of which investors are free to choose any combination they desire. Investors bear the consequences of their choice. The financial intermediary's role is a passive one in the sense that it does not assume the riskiness of the securities it sells.

- *Ability to dispose of bad loans* It is more difficult to dispose of bad loans in a credit-based system than it is in a securities-based system, where secondary markets for securities are developed. This, too, forces banks to establish closer relationships with their corporate clients to assess their soundness and exercise influence in troubled times. Banks may also find themselves forced to lend more when debtor firms run into difficulty, to protect their earlier loans. In securities-based financial systems, investors can easily dispose of their investments on the secondary markets. This possibility allows investors to buy the securities of a firm without getting involved in the firm.

- *Diffusion of power in lending* Bank lending to firms is a personal and centralized one arising from the banks' command of large resources. Furthermore, banks have the resources to monitor their loans and interfere in situations where they feel that there is a need. The banks' decision not to lend to firms in difficult times provides an effective threat.

  In securities-based systems, individual investors naturally command fewer resources than banks. The individual investor's power *vis-à-vis* firms' is diffused by the desire to reduce risk through portfolio diversification, which also reduces the incentive to hold on to non-performing assets, since these assets have a fractional weight in the portfolio. This permits the investors to take fractional losses in the case of the disposition of non-performing assets without any obligation of further commitment.

- *Collateral Requirements* Banks require firms to provide collateral to be eligible for a loan. However justified banks are in trying to protect their loan portfolio, the implication of the collateral requirement is to exclude non-established firms from access to loanable funds. This limits the entry of new firms.

  In a securities-based financial system, investors lend on the basis of prospective return. New firms have access to funds as long as they present profitable alternatives to existing firms. Collateral requirements are not an obstacle in securities-based systems.

Given the characteristics of financial systems, we can discuss the availability of funds to potential entrants and its implication for firm behaviour.

In securities-based financial systems, potential entrants will have access to investable funds as long as they present a profitable asset for investors' portfolios. This requires that they show that they are a profitable alternative to incumbent firms in terms of return and risk. This is possible only if new entrants are at least as efficient as incumbent firms in technological innovation, cost structure and their ability to produce higher quality products. These conditions constitute a list of minimum requirements for entry – new firms will not attempt to enter an industry unless they meet these conditions.

There are two implications of the availability of funds to new entrants for the incumbent firms. First it leads the incumbent firms to rely on internal funds given that potentially successful challenges from new entrants may diminish the possibility of raising funds on the capital markets. In securities-based financial systems, exit from financial holdings is easy through well-developed secondary markets. In troubled times, investors will dispose of the securities of the incumbent firms in favour of successful new entrants, making it very difficult for incumbent firms to obtain funds when they are most needed. Banks will abstain from getting into long-term relationships with firms because banks are vulnerable to the same forces in the presence of well-developed capital markets.

Second, the availability of funds to new entrants means that potentially successful challenges have a high probability of being realized. This forces incumbent firms to maintain their efficiency advantage at all times which in turn implies a strong technological push. This will be reflected in firms' search for new products, better quality products or new production processes through investment expenditures, especially *R&D* expenditures.

The close relationships between banks and firms that arise from the nature of the financial intermediation process in credit-based financial systems have different implications for firm behaviour. In credit-based financial systems, potential entrants present challenges not only to existing firms but also to the banks associated with them. Successful entry undermines the security of past loans. This will lead to credit rationing to potential entrants and further lending to incumbents to improve their competitive position. Consequently, the risk of bankruptcy is reduced because of the availability of funds to firms in troubled times. Firms tend to rely on borrowing more in credit-based systems.

The reduced threat of entry in credit-based financial systems reduces the pressure on incumbent firms to innovate against a potential challenge. There is a tendency to undertake investments that are less risky than usually suggested by technological innovation. Banks are likely to encourage this attitude since technological innovations are riskier investments than they would like to finance. The Japanese success in process and production technology relative to their success in product innovations relies on the fact that innovations in process technologies are less risky than new product designs. Given the proven products on world markets, Japanese banks have been more than eager to finance process innovations that enabled Japanese firms to attain low costs and high quality as, for instance, with colour televisions and video-cassette recorders.

The availability of funds to potential entrants in the credit-based system will also depend on the concentration of financial institutions. If a few major financial institutions dominate the credit-allocation process and are associated with firms in an industry, entry may not be significant or exist at all. In a less concentrated economy, potential entrants may have access to loanable funds through banks that are not already associated with any firm in that industry. However, even when the concentration in the banking sector is low, 'the fallacy of composition effect' may affect the availability of funds to potential entrants. That is, if few banks extend credit to a sector, the profitability of the investment may justify the loans. When more banks lend to the same sector, they may not only hurt the profitability of the initial banks but also the late entrants.

It is important to note that the concentration of financial institutions in securities-based financial systems may not affect the availability of funds to potential entrants. Capital is directly provided by investors and the presence of potential entrants provides an opportunity for adding another asset to the portfolio of investors. The role of financial intermediaries is limited to facilitate the firms' access to surplus funds. The profitability of financial intermediaries increases as they intermediate more.

Finally, as a result of different financing in different systems, the macroeconomic availability of funds is also affected. In the direct mode of financing, firms' heavy reliance on internal funds will free the economy-wide sources for the benefit of potential entrants. Thus, the economy-wide availability of sources will be relatively high for the potential entrants. On the other hand, firms' dependence on credit in the indirect mode of financing will absorb most of the available economy-wide sources, leaving very little or none for potential entrants. That is, in credit-based systems a credit rationing tendency will be felt more keenly.

Direct and Indirect Modes of Financing: Empirical Evidence for the USA, Japan, and Germany

While the descriptive analysis below shows the qualitative differences in the financial structures of the three countries, there are several measures which can be used to distinguish these systems quantitatively. The ratio of loans and securities to total external financing indicates the predominant mode of finance. In credit-based financial systems, firms depend on bank borrowing for their financial sources; in securities-based systems, firms issue bonds and equities to meet their financial needs.

Table 6.1 shows that bank borrowing dominates external financing in Germany and Japan; capital markets are insignificant as a source of external funding. In the USA, on the contrary, capital markets are a major source of finance; securities are close to half of all external financial sources raised. Bank borrowing is limited to short-term borrowing. The descriptive analyses in each country below show that banks are closely involved in capital-market transactions in Germany and Japan but restricted by law in the USA.

A second type of quantitative criterion is the size of capital markets in each country, measured by the value of securities as a share of GDP. Table 6.2 shows that capital markets are

Table 6.1   Sources of external funds of industrial undertaking (percentage)

	Germany (1968–73)	Japan (1970–76)	USA (1970–76)
Loans	60	56.1	29.8
Bonds	4	2.5	33.1
Shares	6	5.3	15.7
Other[1]	30	36.1	21.4
Total	100	100	100

[1]Others include an increase in trade credits received, an increase in other accounts payable, and an increase in the provision for staff superannuation.

Sources: For Germany, B.T. Baylis A.A.S. Butt Phillip (1980), *Capital Markets and Industrial Investment in Germany and France.* Table 2.2 For Japan and the USA, *OECD Financial Statistics 1979.*

Table 6.2 *Value of outstanding securities as a proportion of gross domestic product, end 1978*

	Bonds (%)	Equities (%)
Germany	41%	6%
Japan	54%	9%
USA	58%	49%

Source: OECD Financial Statistics (for the value of outstanding securities) and *OECD National Accounts* (for GDP).

most important in the USA, especially equity markets. In Germany and Japan, industrial firms meet close to two-thirds of their financial needs through loans. The relative importance of bond markets in Germany and Japan arises from government participation in such markets.

These two measures indicate clearly the dominance of capital markets in the USA and loan markets in Japan and Germany. The brief review of financial systems in Germany, Japan and the USA below presents the institutional aspects that produce the results given by the quantitative indicators.

Germany[3]

Basic financial institutions
The German financial system is dominated by the so-called universal banks. These provide a range of financial services that include short-term and long-term lending, underwriting securities, direct investments in other firms, and foreign business. The universal banks draw their financial resources from time deposits, saving certificates and bank bonds. Investing institutions, such as life-insurance companies and pension funds, and special credit institutions play a relatively minor role in the financial system. There is a well-developed market in bonds, but here also the banking sector occupies a dominant position, some banks being the main issuers and others the main purchasers of bonds. The equity market contributes little to industrial finance.

Universal banks   There are three groups of universal banks in Germany: commercial banks, savings banks and credit co-operatives. These groups differ from each other in their legal form, forms of ownership and their aims, but compete with each other as universal banks in all sections of the financial market.

The commercial banks are of four types: big banks, regional banks, private banking firms and the branches of foreign banks. They are private law corporations under the ownership of private individuals or firms, and are profit-oriented in their operations. The most important commercial banks are the Big Three: the Deutsche Bank, the Dresdner Bank and the CommerzBank. The Big Three have national networks of branches. They also have controlling interest or major participation in many other types of financial institution. Their share of claims and liabilities with the non-financial sector is 7 per cent and 8 per cent respectively.[4] But the real influence of the Big Three is executed through their interests in other institutions. The big banks have a much greater significance than their market shares would suggest.

Regional banks are commercial banks that are confined to distinct geographical areas. Nonetheless, some of them, especially the Bavarian Limited Liability Banks (the Bayerische Hypotheken Vereinsbank), have spread across the whole of what was the Federal Republic and also abroad since the 1960s. Their classification as regional banks actually reflects the concentration of their branch network in a particular region. Their combined share of claims and liabilities with the non-financial sector is 8 per cent and 6 per cent respectively.

Private banks specialize in the securities business and investment management. They are organized in the form of partnerships or sole proprietorships. Their value of business is the smallest among the commercial banks. Foreign banks are involved in the business of trade finance and in serving the German subsidiaries of foreign companies.

Savings banks and their central giro institutions are public-law institutions under state ownership and pursue public purposes such as encouraging saving, providing credit for those with low incomes and meeting finance needs of local communities. The individual savings banks are restricted in the business they can do, by being both confined to certain regions and prevented from engaging in certain financial activities, such as investing in securities. But the central giro institutions into which they are grouped at the regional level are not subject to these restrictions and compete in all markets as universal banks. There are 12 such institutions, the largest of which, the Westdeustche Landes-bank in Girozentra, ranks in size with the Big Three commercial banks. The savings banks account altogether for 22 per cent of the liabilities and 16 per cent of the claims of the non-financial sector, while the corresponding shares of the central giro institutions are 7 per cent and 13 per cent respectively. As a group, they account for 29 per cent of both claims and liabilities.

The credit co-operatives are geared towards the interests of their members. Like saving banks, they have joined together to form 12 regional central institutions and a very important national central institution which has become a major bank in both the domestic and international markets.

In addition to the universal banks, there are several credit institutions with specialized functions. These fall into three categories: those concerned with financing public and private construction activity; those which undertake specialized public projects; and those involved in the granting of consumer credit.

Capital markets   Capital markets do not play an important role in the flow of funds to industry in Germany. Their relatively undeveloped nature is explained by the dominance of bank lending in industrial financing. Even though the German market for new security issues is substantial, a large part of new issues is held to maturity by their first buyers (Hennings 1981). Secondary markets are narrow. There is much less trade in bonds and shares outstanding than one would expect from the volume of new issues of securities. In fact, the stock exchange turnover was around 6 per cent of securities outstanding in 1979 (Hennings 1981, Tables 2.4–2.6).

An important feature of the German securities markets is that they are dominated by banks. Not only do banks issue a sizeable quantity of securities, they also hold a considerable number of other banks' securities. The growing importance of the bond market is due to the increase in governmental debt.

Relations with industry

Relations between the German banks and industry are very close as a result of the industrial companies' dependence on the banks for external finance and by the banks' significant industrial holdings. The dominance of universal banks in the German financial system leads all routes to corporate external finance – equity, bonds and loans – back to the banks. To protect their assets, banks are involved closely in the activities of the industrial firms. This involvement is strengthened by the banks' legal right to own stock in corporations and to exercise proxy votes for other shareholders. As a result, banks have helped the expansion of industry and have taken an active part in arranging mergers and takeovers. A report prepared by the Study Commission of the Finance Ministry in 1979 showed that with respect to the 74 large enterprises quoted on the stock exchange in 1974–5, credit institutions in aggregate owned 9 per cent of the capital stock, represented on the average more than 62 per cent of the votes in the stockholders' meeting and held 18 per cent of the seats on the supervisory boards (Francke and Hudson 1986: 48).

The close relationship between banks and firms has developed in the historical context of industrialization in the nineteenth century and the reconstruction efforts after World War II. In the 1970s, banks also became involved in certain firms in the public interest, either to save jobs or to prevent foreign interests from obtaining a majority stake in German firms. In this environment, the availability of funds to new entrants is diminished.

Japan

Basic financial institutions

The Japanese financial system is dominated by the 13 city banks. The city banks are direct descendants of the *zaibatsu* banks, the financial groups of the 1930s. Dissolution of the

Zaibatsu banks after World War II, under the occupation regime, transformed them into today's city banks or group banks. City banks control slightly less than one-third of the financial resources of all financial institutions (down from one-half in the early 1950s) and 60 per cent of the funds of all commercial banks. Six of the city banks form the nuclei of large industrial groupings, giving them a very close bond with group members. Although personal and small-business customers are becoming increasingly important, city banks focus primarily on large-scale enterprises. Their relationship with industrial firms is extremely close, and banks will generally take an active interest in firms' management and would expect firms to discuss major proposals with their group bank before taking a decision.

Local banks are generally smaller than the city banks. They are permitted the same range of activities as city banks but their business is usually concentrated in one prefecture. Their loan customers tend to be small or medium-size local enterprises. They are active lenders in the call market, chanelling liquidity to the city banks.

Three credit banks – the Industrial Bank of Japan, the Long-Term Credit Bank of Japan and the Nippon Credit Bank – provide long-term loans for corporate expansion. These banks can accept deposits from borrowers and the government but not from the general public. Their main source of finance is the issue of debentures.

The seven trust banks also fall into the category of long-term credit banks. They operate as commercial banks but must keep their trust and commercial banking activities separate. Their financing comes largely from loan trusts in which certificates are sold to the public, and become in effect long-term deposits. Their investment activities have been mainly in lending for industrial plant expansion and, more recently, in the purchase of bonds.

The Japanese Postal Savings System, with more than 22,000 branches, plays a major role as a deposit-taking institution. The assets of the Postal Savings System are administered by the government Trust Fund Bureau which mainly invests in government bonds and institutions.

There are many other specialized public and private financial institutions which play an important role in their market niche (such as small-business or securities firms).

Capital markets   Capital markets in Japan do not play a significant role in raising funds for industry. Several factors have kept them from developing. Within each business group (*Keiretsu*) each company owns a certain percentage of other members' stock and group banks act as treasurers of the group. *Keiretsu* banks provide group financing needs and reduce the need to seek funds from outside the group. In effect, the various groups operate their own internal money markets. Firms rely on borrowing from their group banks as indicated by Table 6.1.

The existence of intragroup financial markets managed by a group bank has held back the development of bond markets. The group banks sought to promote debt financing through loans rather than bonds. The administered interest-rate structure kept the demand for bonds low relative to long-run deposits. Until the large government budget deficits of the 1970s forced a partial regulation of interest rates, both private and public bond markets remained thin and shallow.

The bond market is an important source of funds for the public sector and the long-term credit banks. Government bonds are largely held by the Bank of Japan, the Trust Fund Bureau and other financial institutions. The only bonds held in any quantity by the general public are the one-year discount debentures of the long-term credit banks.

Relations with industry

The close relations between industry and banks in Japan depend on the existence of group banks. Banks provide all the financial funds that firms need. This financial support is augmented by management involvement. Banks try to make sure that the firms they support stay competitive in the marketplace. Firms are expected to consult with their group banks before they make a major move. As a result, firms are sure of financial help in bad times, as long as management convinces the group banks that the firm can compete successfully after overcoming its financial difficulties.

Even where a group relationship does not prevail, one of the usually numerous banks from which large corporations borrow is regarded as its main bank and, as such, has a special responsibility towards the borrower. In an emergency, other creditors can expect their claims to be paid back before those of the main bank.

Both Caves and Uekusa (1976) and Wallich and Wallich (1976) point out the explicit discrimination that exists against small firms in the financial markets. Caves and Uekusa note that corporations with equity capital of less than 10 million Yen incur 50 per cent higher costs than firms with capital of more than 1 billion Yen. Wallich and Wallich argue that small firms that are marginally attached to a group or independent do not benefit from the advantages that apply to group firms. These advantages range from help from the lead bank in arranging loans to postponement of payments to other group firms.

The United States

The US financial system can be characterized as segmented by law and dominated by capital markets. The deposit-taking institutions are specialized and have been legally prevented from engaging in investment banking and from holding corporate securities. Regulation of the financial system in the USA was slow to develop. The cycles of bank failures finally led to the emergence of a regulatory structure aimed at limiting 'excessive competition'. The result has been the segmentation of deposit-taking institutions. There is a complicated two-tier structure of banking supervision by federal and state authorities with overlapping duties.

Deposit-taking institutions include the commercial banks, mutual savings banks, savings and loan associations and credit unions. Commercial banks in the USA are regulated by a dual system of federal and state control. National banks are chartered and supervised by the Comptroller of the Currency and state banks by the state banking authorities. Membership of the Federal Reserve System is compulsory for the national

Table 6.3   Share in total deposits at the five largest banks

West Germany (1980)	61.8%
Japan (1981)	34.5%
United States (1981)	19.2%

Source: Dwight Crane, 1983, Exhibit 3.

banks but optional for the state banks. All member banks have to join the Federal Deposit Insurance Corporation (FDIC), but non-members may also join the FDIC, in which case some of their activities are regulated by the latter.

There are presently about 15,000 commercial banks in the USA, and about 13,000 have total assets of US $50 million or less. Although the regulatory policies against mergers and branching are the primary reason for such a large number of banks, 42 per cent of all bank assets in 1979 were held by 0.2 per cent of the banks (33 banks). Over 60 per cent of all bank assets were held by the 186 banks with total assets in excess of US-$1 billion.[5] Yet, the US banking seems to be less concentrated than the West German or Japanese (Table 6.3).

Branching laws for all banks are determined by the state in which they are located. These effectively eliminate inter-state branching. This prohibition has become less restrictive as a result of the development of bank-holding companies.

Over half the assets of the commercial banks are in the form of loans, about a quarter are in public-sector securities and the rest are in cash and bank deposits.[6] One-third of bank loans are to industry and commerce, usually on a short-term basis; a quarter are in the form of commercial and residential mortgages; and the majority of the remainder are consumer loans for instalment purchases. More than half of the liabilities take the form of time deposits and savings accounts, and about one-quarter are in the form of demand deposits. The commercial banks account for one-third of the liabilities and claims with the non-financial sector.

Savings and loan associations, mutual savings banks and credit unions are depository institutions that deal with households. These institutions specialize in offering savings and time accounts to households. They invest in real-estate finance with the bulk of their business devoted to providing mortgage loans. They engage in a limited amount of short-term lending to consumers and businesses. Mutual savings banks are also involved in real-estate finance, but a substantial portion of their assets is in the form of loans of various maturities to businesses, and they hold a limited amount of corporate stock. Credit unions specialize in providing short-term consumer loans to their members.

Investing institutions   Insurance companies, pension funds, mutual funds and real estate investment funds are an important part of the USA financial system. Together they account for one-third of the liabilities and claims with the non-financial sector. Most of the investments of these institutions are in corporate securities.

Capital markets   The USA's capital markets are the largest and most developed in the world. They are an important source of funds for most categories of borrowers, including federal, state and local government, long-term credit institutions and the corporate sector. Corporations are the major suppliers of securities on the capital markets, bonds the leading form of financing. Both government and corporation securities are held mainly by commercial banks and households, but the importance of the insurance companies and pension funds has been increasing dramatically at the expense of other sectors.

Relations with industry
Relations between commercial banks and industry are limited for regulatory and structural reasons: commercial banks in the USA are prohibited from equity participation in industrial companies. When bankers sit on the boards of companies, they do so in their own right, not as bank representatives; firms raise most of their external funds through capital markets. The banks' role is usually limited to short-term lending. In this capacity, the banks' relationship to industry is

arm's length and short-term.

The most important implication of the limited nature of the bank-industry relation in the USA is the absence of a heavy bias in favour of existing firms, as one finds in Germany or Japan. New firms are provided with the funds they need as long as they present profitable opportunities for investors.

Empirical Evidence on the Impact of Financial Systems: A Comparative Perspective

Our brief survey of the financial systems of the USA, Japan and Germany permits two types of empirical observations:

- The conditions for the availability of capital to potential entrants are easy to fulfill in the securities-based financial system of the USA relative to Germany and Japan.
- In the securities-based financial system of the USA, funds in the form of risk capital are abundant, again relative to Germany and Japan, providing a financial basis for technological innovation.

Direct evidence that will further support the first empirical observation is impossible to present since banks are not required to gather and publish reports about the firms they lend to. Even if detailed data were made available, they would not take into account the discouraged entrants. The importance of the availability of funds in the securities-based systems is to encourage potential entrants to exploit existing profit opportunities.

A comparison of the industry concentration ratios may substitute for direct evidence. Such a comparison across countries and industries provides empirical evidence for the availability of funds in different financial systems without having the disadvantage of omitting discouraged entrants. If funds are easily available in one financial system relative to another, then we would expect the concentration ratios to be lower in countries where funds are readily available. For example, as Caves and Uekusa (1976) note, the interest-rate differences that favour large firms in Japan cause artificial economies for large-scale enterprises and tend to make firms larger and markets more concentrated than they need be. Concentration-ratio comparisons overcome the problem of omitting the discouraged entrants and the firms which are denied access to funds.

An obvious problem with the comparison of concentration ratios is that economic factors other than the nature of the financial systems may also be important in determining the differences in those ratios. To that extent, the explanatory power of using concentration ratios as an indicator of capital availability will be reduced. One would expect, however, that many important variables, such as technology, efficient plant size and market size, are common across the countries studied here. The large domestic market of the USA is matched by the export orientation of the German and Japanese economies which compensates for their smaller home markets. As regards the governments' competition policies, in both Germany and Japan such policies were influenced by the USA's approach in the period following World War II. However, it can be argued that in the context of their development process the German and Japanese governments have been less vigorous in their anti-trust policies than the US government.[7] Such policy differences among the governments certainly account for some of the differences in the concentration ratios across the countries.

The concentration ratio data across countries are collected by the Committee of Experts on Restrictive Business Practices of the OECD and published in its report on 'Concentration and Competition Policy'.[8] The collected data are not uniform across countries. The data for Germany are 3-firm concentration ratios, whereas for the USA they are 4-firm and for Japan, 5-firm. The non-disclosure rules in Germany prevent publication of more detailed data (see Table 6.4).

Since the German data are 3-firm concentration ratios, the German concentration is understated relative to the other countries; on the other hand, the Japanese 5-firm concentration ratio is overstated relative to the others. A clear picture emerges from Table 6.5. The percentage of industries characterized as very high to high is 59 per cent in the USA for a 4-

Table 6.4   *Concentration ratios in the USA, Japan and Germany*

Concentration ratio	USA[1]	Japan[2]	Germany[3]
90 and over	12	45	–
80 to 89.9	10	23	–
70 to 79.9	22	21	–
60 to 69.9	29	21	41
50 to 59.9	54	17	–
40 to 49.9	60	21	–
30 to 39.9	67	12	56
20 to 29.9	95	5	–
10 to 19.9	66	4	49
under 10	14	1	10
Total number of industries	429	170	156

[1] Four-firm concentration ratios, value of shipments
[2] Five-firm concentration ratios, production (1970)
[3] Three-firm concentration ratios, sales

Source: OECD *Concentration and Competition Policy*, 1979, Tables 2.7 and 2.13.

firm concentration, where as it is 94 per cent in Japan for a 5-firm concentration and 62 per cent in Germany for a 3-firm concentration ratio.

The second set of empirical evidence is related to both the capital-availability and risk-capital hypotheses. If potential entrants have easy access to capital, they will enter the industry if they are at least as efficient as the incumbent firms. This forces the incumbent firms to maintain their efficiency advantages at all times, which implies strong technological dynamics in the industry. Firms, incumbent or new entrants, will continuously introduce new products and new production techniques to stay competitive. The degree of technological dynamics in the industry can be measured by the ratio of *R&D* expenditures to investments. As discussed in Chapter 5, the *R&D/I* ratio reflects the technological dynamics of an industry

Table 6.5 Concentration ratios in the USA, Japan and Germany (%)

Industry groups:	USA	Japan	Germany
very high concentration	0.29	0.75	0.263
high concentration	0.30	0.19	0.36
medium concentration	0.38	0.05	0.314
low concentration	0.03	0.01	0.064
Total	1.00	1.00	1.00

Note: The figures from Table 6.4 are aggregated under the German Monopolies Commission characterization with concentration ratios of 50 per cent and over as having very high concentration, of 25–50 per cent as having high concentration, of 10–25 per cent as having medium concentration and of under 10 per cent as having low concentration.

Source: See Table 6.4.

Table 6.6 Technological dynamics in manufacturing industry in the USA, Germany and Japan (1979)

	R&D/Domestic product of industry (%)	R&D/I(%)
USA	6.5	67.2
Germany	4.0	32.7
Japan	3.7	22.1

Source: OECD *Science and Technology Indicators Resources Devoted to R&D*, OECD, Paris, 1984: 57, Table 1.7.

more accurately than the conventional *R&D*/sales ratio. The hypothesis on the availability of capital can be restated as follows: the technological dynamics of the industry, measured by the *R&D*/Investment ratio, ought to be higher in the USA with its capital-market finance than in Japan and Germany with their credit-based financial systems. The empirical evidence is presented in Table 6.6.

As seen from Table 6.6, the *R&D/I* ratio in the USA is triple that of Japan and more than double that of Germany. The availability of funds to potential entrants in the USA forces the incumbent firms to innovate continuously to keep their technological lead. In Germany and Japan the incumbent firms are not under such pressure since credit availability to potential entrants is relatively restricted. In a recent study of the Japanese corporation, Abegglen and Stalk (1985) support the view that the financial institutions in Japan do not like taking risks. The authors conclude that:

the evidence in Japan shows that financial institutions are taking few risks. Until very recently, Japanese financial institutions only lent money against collateral whose values are very much understated on their balance sheets. These assets include land, marketable securities and long-term receivables. The existence of these assets reduces the financial risks of many *kaisha* which aggressively use debt to fund their growth. (1985: 15)

Potential entrants in the USA are able to challenge incumbent firms through technological innovation because the capital markets in the USA provide the risk capital necessary to finance risky innovation. Investors are compensated by higher rates of returns for riskier investments. In credit-based financial systems such as in Japan or Germany, tests of creditworthiness are too stringent for new ventures, demanding security and/or a trade record rather than analysing the market prospects. As equity holders in large companies, the German and Japanese banks are tied to the existing firms.

The availability of risk capital in the USA relative to Japan and Germany can be measured by the size of venture capital in each country. Venture capital is a source of risk capital in its purest form. Investors provide capital to new firms to exploit the risky opportunities with the knowledge that they may never get their initial capital back. Returns on the venture are realized by selling the stocks on the capital markets if the venture in which they invested proves to be successful.

The size of US venture capital in the early 1980s exceeded US \$10 billion, far surpassing Japan (about US \$130 million) and Germany (about US \$300 million). There are more than 500 venture capital firms in the USA, compared with about 30 in Japan (20 started since early 1982) and 6 in Germany (5 of these have been announced since June 1983).[9] The massive equity markets in the USA, and the over-the-counter market in particular, provide liquidity to investors that the thin equity markets in Japan and Germany cannot offer.

THE IMPACT OF FINANCIAL SYSTEMS ON THE TECHNOLOGICAL DYNAMICS AND FINANCING PATTERNS OF FIRMS ACROSS COUNTRIES: AN EMPIRICAL ASSESSMENT

In this section, the hypotheses suggested above (pp. 133–5) are tested econometrically for the OECD countries for which data were available. The first hypothesis is that in the securities-based financial systems, the availability of capital to potential entrants forces incumbent firms to be technologically efficient at all times. The technological dynamics of firms in securities-based countries are relatively higher than those in credit-based financial systems. This is also because of the relative abundance of risk capital in the securities-based financial systems. The second hypothesis states that it is the availability of capital, which is determined by the institutional structure of the financial systems, rather than the cost of capital that determines firms' financing decisions. The relative availability of capital to potential entrants through capital markets induces firms to rely on internal funds in the securities-based financial systems.

To test these hypotheses, first, the financial systems are classified in terms of the importance of long-term direct financing relative to long-term indirect financing in firms' investment decisions. Only long-term financing is taken into consideration because short-term borrowing is usually for firms' working capital needs rather than capital investment needs. The measure for long-term direct financing is the sum of the annual issuance of stocks and bonds. For indirect financing, long-term borrowing from banks and other institutions is used. If the long-term direct financing is dominant, that is, if

$$\frac{\text{Long-term bonds} + \text{stocks } (S)}{\text{Long-term bank borrowing } (B)} > 1$$

Table 6.7   The nature of financial systems in ten OECD countries (averages of 1977–81 or the latest available years)

Country	S/B
United States	3.42
Japan	0.94
France	0.49
United Kingdom	3.34
Canada	1.45
Netherlands	0.47
Sweden	1.00
Norway	0.26
Denmark	0.65
Finland	0.15

Source: OECD, *Financial Statistics Part 3*: Non-Financial Enterprises–Financial Statements, 1985.

then the country's financial system can be characterized as a securities-based financial system. If the ratio of long-term bonds plus stocks to long-term bank borrowing is less than one, the financial system of the country can be classified as a credit-based system.

Table 6.7 presents the data on the nature of financial systems for ten OECD countries for which data are available. The data are averages for the period 1977–81, or the latest available years. As seen from Table 6.7, there are significant differences in the financial systems of the countries in question. While the ratio of long-term direct financing to long-term indirect financing is 3.42 in the USA, the same ratio falls to as low as 0.15 for Finland. There are four countries with the ratio of long-term direct financing to indirect financing equal to or greater than one, which can be classified as securities-based systems according to this indicator. These countries are the USA, the UK, Canada and Sweden. Other countries have ratios less than one (it should be kept in mind that the data are for the period of 1977–81). In the rapidly-changing conditions of the world economy, especially the internationalization of the financial markets, these ratios change continuously and most probably in favour of direct financing in the face of rapid securitization all over the world.

Financial Systems and Technological Dynamics

According to the hypothesis suggested above (p. 151), the structure of the financial system influences the technological dynamics of an economy. In securities-based financial systems, the availability of funds to new entrants means that potentially successful challenges have a high probability of being realized. This forces incumbent firms to maintain their efficiency advantage at all times which, in turn, induces a strong technological push by industry.

In credit-based systems, the reduced threat of entry lessens the pressure on existing firms to innovate against a potential challenge. There is a tendency to undertake investments that are less risky than is usually suggested by technological innovation. Banks are likely to encourage these since technological innovations are riskier investments for them also.

The degree of technological dynamics in an industry is measured by the ratio of *R&D* expenditures, excluding those supported by the government, to investment expenditures (I) in the business sector. The empirical evidence is presented in Table 6.8 which shows that the *R&D/I* ratio is the highest in the USA whereas it is lowest in Finland. The availability of funds to potential entrants in the USA forces incumbent firms to innovate continuously to keep their technological lead.

Using the least-squares method, the following regression equation is tested to find out the importance of the type of financial system on technological dynamics for the countries for which data are available:

$$R\&D/I = \alpha + \beta\, S/B + \epsilon_t$$

where

$R\&D/I$ = the ratio of research and development expenditures

Table 6.8   *The technological dynamics in manufacturing indus-*
                try in ten OECD countries (1979)

Country	R&D/I (%)
United States	67.2
Japan	22.1
France	19.4
United Kingdom	35.6
Canada	12.2
Netherlands	26.1
Sweden	31.8
Norway	13.9
Denmark	19.7
Finland	7.9

Source: See Table 6.6.

to the investment expenditures in the business sector. This is a measure of the technological dynamics of the economy

S/B = the ratio of direct financing (stocks + bonds) to indirect financing (bank borrowing) as a measure of the type of financial structure in the economy
ϵ_t = error term

It is expected that both the coefficient of the variable used as the measure of the financial structure of the economy and the explanatory power of the equation will be significant.

With all ten countries included, the above regression was estimated as

$$R\&D/I = 11.8 + 11.3\, S/B$$
$$\quad\quad (2.39) \quad\quad (3.80)$$

with t-statistics given in the parentheses. The coefficient of the finance variable is significant at the 99.5 per cent level, whereas the coefficient of the intercept is significant at the 95.6 per cent level. R^2 = 64.4 per cent and the adjusted R^2 = 59.8 per cent, where R^2 is the coefficient of determination.

When we run the regression equation excluding outliers, Canada and the Netherlands, the estimated equation is

$$R\&D/I = 11.7 + 12.1 \, S/B$$
$$(2.37) \quad (4.37)$$

The coefficient of the financial system is still significant at the 99.5 per cent level, while the significance level of the coefficient of the intercept falls to 94.4 per cent. The R^2 rises to 76 per cent and the adjusted R^2 to 72 per cent.

Even though the results are dependent upon data which require cautious interpretation, these results support the hypothesis that the structure of the financial system plays a significant role in influencing the technological dynamics of the economy as it is expounded.

In evaluating the performance of financial systems, the financial markets' impact on technological dynamics should be taken into account.[10] As these dynamics are becoming an increasingly important determinant of competitiveness in the world economy, the selection of direct instead of indirect financing becomes ever more critical.

Financial Systems and Financing Patterns Across Countries

Empirical evidence presented in Table 1.2 in Chapter 1 shows that there are significant variations in financing patterns across countries. Firms in the USA and UK finance themselves through their internal funds. The ratio of internal financing is close to 90 per cent in the USA and UK, whereas it stays between 60–70 per cent in other countries. There is a striking causal observation that can be seen from the data as regards the institutional nature of the financial systems that exist in these countries. The securities-based systems of the USA and UK, which are considered to be the most developed systems, have made the lowest net funding contributions. In the credit-based financial systems, firms have financed higher proportions of investments through external funds.

The corporate finance theory based on Modigliani and Miller's (1958) proposition of the irrelevance of corporate finance fails to account for the differences in funding patterns across countries. There are two crucial assumptions of the Modigliani–Miller framework that constitute intellectual stumbling-blocks in explaining financing patterns across countries: the separation of investment and finance; and the negligence of the role of financial institutions in explaining financing patterns across countries.

Finance theories have emphasized taxation as the main influence on corporate capital structures across countries. Studies analysing the role of taxation, however, could find little relationship between financing patterns and taxation (Mayer 1988, Rutterford 1988). Most recently, Mayer (1988) ranked tax wedges in the United States, Britain, Germany and Japan for retentions, debt and new debt–equity finance. He found that taxation did not explain the rankings of the debt/retention proportions.

The differences in the cost of capital between the USA and Japan are not significant enough to account for the relatively large dependence on internal funds in the USA. When the effective tax rates are taken account, as the empirical evidence presented by Nakatani (1986) and reproduced in Table 6.9 shows, the cost of capital in the USA is lower than in Japan. The cost of capital data given in Table 6.9 take into account both the average cost of funds and the effective tax rate. The former is usually lower in Japan than in the USA because Japanese interest rates have been generally lower than those of the USA. However, effective tax rates are much higher in Japan, reducing the differences in costs of capital between the two countries.

The conclusion that can be derived from the debt/taxation literature is striking: the cost of capital is not the main determinant of the capital structure. Any analysis of financing patterns needs to address this unorthodox result.

Recent developments in neoclassical economics have emphasized the asymmetries of information and the insider–outsider distinction in corporate financing decisions (Edwards 1987, and Mayer 1988). Mayer has been an exception in attempting directly to explain financing patterns across countries.

Table 6.9   Cost of capital in Japan and the USA

	Machinery and equipment		Structure	
	Japan	USA	Japan	USA
1975	21.1	25.7	7.1	12.6
1976	22.0	24.7	8.2	11.3
1977	24.5	23.6	11.4	10.0
1978	24.0	21.3	11.0	7.0
1979	20.7	21.3	6.9	7.0
1980	24.6	24.9	11.5	11.1
1981	26.6	24.8	13.7	15.0
1982	27.0	24.5	14.2	14.9
1983	26.9	23.0	14.0	13.3

Source: Nakatani 1986: 129, Table 3.

Mayer presents an explanation that is based on the long-term relationship between banks and firms. He argues that competitive financial markets discourage long-term relationships which are important for external finance. His analysis depends on the problem of time inconsistency: *ex-ante*, a long-term relationship may be optimal, but *ex-post* the firm or the lenders have the incentive to renege. Competitive financial markets provide opportunities to exit and prevent long-term relationships from developing. Mankiw (1988), however, mentions that as long as firms can write contracts to cover the most important contingencies, precommitment should also be possible in the presence of competitive financial markets; or, as Barroux (1988) argues, if firms renege, the reputation of not being dependable will bear on possible future loans.

Even though Mayer presents the issue as a time-inconsistency problem, he actually touches upon one of the most important aspects of financial systems in explaining financing patterns. This is the possibility of easy 'exit' in securities-based systems. The other aspects of financial systems considered in the earlier parts of this book blended the competitive nature of the investment process with the financial structure of the economy.

One hypothesis of this study is that the institutional structure of financial systems influences the financing patterns of
firms. In securities-based financial systems, capital markets
that provide funds to successful entrants may refuse to extend
capital to unsuccessful incumbents, thus endangering their
survival. Firms faced with uncertainty about the availability
of funds in the competitive process rely on internal funds. In
credit-based financial systems, since bank loans predominate
the financial intermediation process, entry becomes more difficult. Close relationships between firms and banks in such
systems increase the availability of financial funds to incumbent firms, inducing them to rely on bank-borrowing.

To test the hypothesis, the following regression equation is
measured using the least-squares method for the countries
where data is available:

$$IF/I = a + b\,S/B + \epsilon_t$$

where

IF/I = the ratio of internal funds to investments in non-financial assets; this is a measure of financing patterns
S/B = the ratio of long-term bonds plus stocks (S) to long-
term borrowing (B); this variable measures the institutional
nature of the financial system in the economy

ϵ_t = error term

With all the nine countries included, the above regression is
estimated as

$$IF/I = 61.9 + 7.75\,S/BB$$
$$\quad\;\;(21.02)\quad\;(4.54)$$

with t-statistics given in the parentheses. The coefficient of the
financial institution is highly significant and $R^2 = 74.6$ per
cent and the adjusted $R^2 = 71.0$ per cent, where the R^2 is the
coefficient of determination. These results support the hypothesis that the structure of the financial system plays an import-

ant role in affecting the financing patterns of firms across countries.

Financial systems are distinguished by the availability of capital to potential entrants. In securities-based systems, capital is available to successful entrants but not to unsuccessful incumbents. In credit-based systems, the close relationships between banks and firms provide incumbents with access to capital while restricting access for potential entrants. Once the capital availability aspect of financial systems is taken into account, variations in financing patterns can be explained as the regression analysis shows.

NOTES

1. See Cameron (1972) for historical evidence on the Gershenkron hypothesis.
2. Feldman (1986).
3. Discussion in this section draws upon Francke and Hudson (1984), Cable (1985), Vittas (1978), Hennings (1981), Baylis and Buttphilip (1980).
4. Statistics are from Vittas (1978).
5. FDIC Annual Report 1979.
6. Federal Reserve Bulletin, April 1983: 1174.
7. Caves and Uekesa (1976).
8. OECD 'Concentration and Competition Policy Data' (1979).
9. Wellons (1985).
10. Mayer (1987).

7. Competitiveness in the World Economy

The analysis of competition so far has perceived it as an interactive process between firms, financial institutions and the government within national borders. It was important to bring out the essence of the conception of competition as a survival process. For this reason, the unit of analysis at the national economy level was the firm. It was argued that it is the competition between firms that produces continuous technological change which is one of the basic features of the capitalist development process; another feature, as was pointed out in Chapter 1, is the uneven development of regions and nations and the shifts in the centre of power and growth over time. To explain this second feature of capitalist development, the competitive process needs to be studied at the world-economy level. Such an analysis reveals the importance of the interaction between national institutional structures and government policies.

The recent dynamics of the world economy, as reflected in the internationalization of financial markets and the changing nature of competitiveness, is historically unprecedented, in the sense of weakening the independence of national sovereignty. In the past, national policies, such as trade or foreign investment policies, were determined by national governments to advance their interests. When certain policies did not help the promotion of the interests of the countries, they were reversible. For example, the protectionist stance of the USA in the nineteenth century was replaced in favour of free trade in the twentieth century to be shadowed by protectionist tendencies since the early 1970s. However, the changing nature of competitiveness in the world economy together with the internationalization of financial markets shape national policies and present an irreversible process. To take advantage of the recent dynamics of the world economy, national economies are opening up and national governments make concessions from traditional sovereign policy areas. The internationalization of financial markets, for example, reduces the effectiveness of national monetary and credit policies; or, to keep employment in their national borders, governments of industrialized countries compete with each other in offering tax breaks and subsidies.

These recent developments have implications for both nation states and firm behaviour in the world economy. Competitiveness in the world economy has become a central issue in academia, business and political circles throughout the industrialized nations. The urgency of the issue is reflected in the new trade proposals in the US Congress. One fruitful product of these discussions has been the realization of the inadequacy of conventional trade theories in understanding current trade relations. Participants in the discussions have developed new trade theories based on a dynamic comparative advantage determined not by natural resources but by national strategies and institutions.[1] The emphasis on national strategies and institutions has promoted trade and industrial policies based on past experiences. These policies tend to be narrowly nationalistic and lack a vision of the world economy that could secure their expected success. On the other hand, firms make their strategies at the global level and act globally to maintain their competitiveness: the Japanese firms produce cars inside the markets they sell to and take advantage of financial sources on the world financial markets rather than limiting themselves to national borders.

The changing nature of competition demands policies that take into account the dynamics of the world economy. This chapter attempts to explain the policy implications of the internationalization of financial markets and rapid technological change as the two forces that shape those dynamics. Developments in the world economy in the post-World War II period are summarized. The implications of the internationalization of the financial markets is analysed, and the changing nature of competitiveness explained. Policy challenges facing national governments are highlighted and the changes taking place in firms' behaviour, as exemplified by the Japanese firms, are reviewed.

THE WORLD ECONOMY IN PERSPECTIVE[2]

Developments in the international economy in the post-World War II period fall into three periods: from the end of World War II until the late 1960s; from the late 1960s to the early 1980s; and from the early 1980s to the present. The first period witnessed high growth rates in international production and trade, accompanied by stable exchange rates. The Bretton Woods agreements provided the basis for growing prosperity and interdependence in the international economy during this phase. In the second period, the Bretton Woods system became increasingly inadequate and eventually had to be abandoned. Since the fixed exchange-rate system of Bretton Woods came to an end in 1971, the liberalization of international trade has been shadowed by increasing protectionism. While growth rates in international production and trade slowed down, unemployment rates increased. Volatility, rather than stability, became the norm of exchange rates. The most recent period is increasingly characterized by the internationalization of financial markets and rapid technological developments. Competitiveness in the world economy has become the main concern of national governments and firms alike.

Ironically, the demise of Bretton Woods was brought on by its success in achieving the first stage in the integration of the world economy – the internationalization of production. As trade was liberalized through GATT rounds in line with the Bretton Woods agreements, the world markets became increasingly interdependent. The internationalization of production, first pushed by US multinationals to overcome the tariff and geographic barriers of the 1950s, proceeded rapidly through a search for low labour costs in the world economy.

Technological developments allowed off-shore production of labour-intensive parts. The emergence of low labour costs as the determining factor in international competitiveness meant that firms in relatively low labour-cost countries could compete successfully in the standardized-technology industries. The growth of Japanese and European firms, especially in steel, shipbuilding, motor vehicles and consumer electronics, increasingly squeezed the profits of US firms. This led to a decline in manufacturing employment and production in the USA. By the late 1960s, as the European countries and Japan closed the gap with the USA, their position in the world economy changed from being a market for American exports to becoming competitors in the world markets. The emerging structural changes rendered the world economic order established by the Bretton Woods system unsustainable.

These structural changes were reflected in the continual decline in the US share of production and exports, with a corresponding increase in that of West Germany, Japan and the newly industrializing countries (NICs), with South Korea and Brazil as notable examples. These changes have not produced responses to the current economic imbalances that were as constructive as the solutions in 1944, when the United States was the leading country supporting the development of other countries. The establishment of the international monetary system and trade relations drew the common interests of the industrialized countries together. Today, with the resurgence of Japan, Europe and the NICs, the economic power in the world economy is distributed more evenly.

Responses to international imbalances are now based on case studies without any clear vision of international economic relationships. When the exchange-rate fluctuations reach unacceptable dimensions, they are discussed in the meetings of the finance ministers of the five to seven industrialized countries. Trade relations are dealt with by protectionist measures on a product basis, like the textile quotas in various production categories and the 'voluntary' export restraints on Japanese cars and microchips. It is dubious whether these measures do anything beyond increasing uncertainties in the world economy.

Given the difficulties faced by US firms, the decline in high–wage manufacturing employment and the US economic position in the world economy, there have been several policy proposals to reverse the trend of the last two decades. These proposals were presented as 'industrial policies' in the early 1980s and as 'competitiveness' more recently.[3] Government intervention in the economy – akin to what has occurred in Japan and Germany – constitutes the basic thrust of the policies, whose prescriptions range from protection for trade to the channelling of capital funds to certain sectors. These policies try to reverse the declining US position in the world economy without taking the global repercussions into account. Interventionist policies are based on the premise that the future world economic order will simply be an extension of relationships that existed in the last three decades. The internationalization of financial markets and the changing nature of competitiveness have, however, been promoting international economic relationships that are different from the ones perceived by policy-makers. Policies aimed at restoring competitiveness and favourable economic conditions in the world economy must take advantage of these developments to be successful.

FINANCIAL SYSTEMS AND THE INTERNATIONALIZATION OF FINANCIAL MARKETS

Policy discussions have enlightened the role of financial systems in promoting competitiveness. The efficacious use of financial policies by the Japanese government created a favourable impression of credit-based systems.[4] The control of financial policy variables and credit allocation mechanisms by the government and the close relationships that exist between banks and firms created the basis for a belief that credit-based systems are more successful at funding industry than securities-based systems. Policy advised by several academicians both in the United States and Britain emphasized similar intervention in the financial markets. With the inter-

Table 7.1   New lending facilities in international financial markets 1981–5 (in billions of US$)

Facility	1981	1982	1983	1984	1985
International bond issues	44.0	71.7	72.1	108.1	162.8
Note issuance facilities	1.0	2.3	3.3	18.9	49.4
Syndicated Euro-bank Loans	96.5	100.5	51.8	36.6	21.6
Total	141.5	174.5	127.2	163.6	233.8

Source: Bank for International Settlements, *Recent Innovations in International Banking*, Basel 1986: 130.

nationalization of financial markets, however, the so-called advantages of the credit-based systems are eroded and may even become a burden for competitiveness.

Until the late 1970s, international capital flows consisted of direct foreign investment and commercial bank-lending with sovereign financial markets. In the early 1980s, the importance of bank-lending declined substantially. The securitized assets became the dominant component of new lending facilities (Table 7.1). In 1981, of the total new lending facilities of US $141.5 billion, US $96.5 billion were lent through syndicated Euro-bank loans. Four years later in 1985, the bank share declined not only in relative terms, to less than 10 per cent of the new lending facilities, but also in absolute terms, to US $21.6 billion. Over the same time period the share of international bond issues increased from 31 per cent to 70 per cent and to US $162.8 billion.

Sovereign financial markets permitted each country's government to use the markets to promote competitiveness through low interest-rate policies and credit-allocation mechanisms. The ability of governments to use a financial system for competitive purposes depends on the nature of the financial system. In credit-based financial systems, where indirect financing through bank loans dominates financial intermediation, governments could direct funds to desired sectors at a low cost. The limited nature of capital markets in credit-based systems reduces the choice of alternative financial assets to bank deposits for savers. This allows governments to direct savings to bank deposits at low interest rates through interest-rate regulations and/or monetary policies. The centralized nature of financial intermediation through banking institutions permitted effective government intervention, as the Japanese experience showed.[5]

In securities-based systems, the decentralized nature of financial intermediation through capital markets limits the scope and means of government intervention. The financial intermediaries' role is limited to offering a range of assets to investors and sources of finance to firms. Attempts by the government to direct the flow of funds through securities firms restrain the financial intermediation role of those firms, thus hampering an efficient flow of funds between sectors. The use of monetary policies to attract deposits at low interest rates is not operational because it is counteracted by a wide range of assets offered to savers in the capital markets.

The credit-based financial systems of Japan and Germany allowed the governments of these countries to direct the available funds to the desired sectors. Sectoral credit-allocation policies added an advantage to the Japanese firms' competition on the world markets. In the United States and Britain, with their securities-based financial systems, the governments did not use financial markets for competitive purposes.

The internationalization of financial markets eliminates the claimed advantages of the credit-based financial systems, implying the opening of domestic financial markets to foreign financial and non-financial institutions. Investors now have a choice of portfolios composed of worldwide assets. As Japanese savers and pension funds discovered, foreign bonds and stocks became an attractive alternative financial asset to domestic ones. It becomes especially difficult for governments to attract savings to deposit institutions at low interest rates. Control of the financial parameters by governments is weakened.

The internationalization of financial markets changes the relationship between domestic firms and banks, eliminating the so-called advantage of credit-based financial systems at the micro-level. Banks' control of credit allocation in credit-based systems is weakened and the domestic availability of funds is enhanced. Banks are no more the sole providers of funds. Second, banks cannot attract deposits at low rates; consequently, they cannot lend out at low rates to firms, which is to say banks also lose their price advantage.

The close relationships between banks and firms decrease with the opening up of financial markets. Firms facing the challenge of potential entrants rely relatively more on internal funds. External funds that are supportive of the undertaking of technologically innovative investments become preferable to bank credits in the new competitive environment.

In short, the institutional advantages that Japan accrued from government control of the credit-allocation process, and the closeness of the bank–firm relationships in credit-based financial systems, have diminished with the internationalization of financial markets. On the other hand, the depth and diversity of capital markets in securities-based systems bring a competitive edge by attracting worldwide savings. The inflow of funds to such systems increases the availability of investable funds while reducing their costs.

THE CHANGING NATURE OF COMPETITIVENESS

The internationalization of financial markets has been taking place in the midst of another important process: the changing nature of competitiveness in the world economy. There are several forces at work here. The accelerating pace of technological breakthroughs in computers, telecommunications and information processing have been shifting the source of competitiveness from labour costs to technological innovation. The developments in computers and information technology have caused rapid automation in labour-intensive industries. As the American examples of RCA in televisions and Xerox in copiers show, automation brings down production costs below Far-Eastern wages, thus reducing the importance of labour costs as a factor in competitiveness. The development and use of new information technology becomes crucial in determining competitiveness.[6]

The rapidity of technological evolution renders new technological developments obsolete in a short time. The easy transfer of process and product technologies through global telecommunications forces companies to intensify their *R&D* efforts.

The emergence of NICs, such as South Korea and Brazil, with potential to copy new technologies further shortens product cycles. As a result, countries like Japan, which relied on an 'imitation strategy' in the 1950s–60s, find themselves in a vulnerable situation. These countries emphasize *R&D*, which further stimulates rapid technological innovation.[7]

High-growth prospects in information-based industries, such as computers and telecommunications, in contrast to the low-growth rates in traditional manufacturing bring out the importance of factors that promote information-based industries. These factors range from the science and technology infrastructure to the provision of risk capital by the financial system. Thus, the rules of competition in the world economy differ significantly today from the post-World War II period. They favour institutional structures that generate innovation. Centralized institutional structures that proved to be successful in the earlier period may lack the flexibility and versatility required in responding to current changes in the world economy.

POLICY CHALLENGES FACING THE NATIONAL GOVERNMENTS

Given the emergence of the new economic relationships in the world economy, protectionist trade and industrial policies reflect attempts to revive the US economy on the basis of the outmoded relationships of the past. The success of these policies is limited. Rather than bolstering the American competitive position, protectionist trade and industrial policies encourage past relationships which were unfavourable to the

USA. In order to stimulate its competitiveness, the United States should promote an economic environment that is favourable to its firms through the internationalization of financial markets. Policies to restore macroeconomic and international balances will provide conditions for a safe transition.

The new challenge posed by the developments in the world economy is the provision of risk capital to firms. Since firms have to innovate continuously in order to stay competitive, they need risk capital. The depth of the capital markets encourages the growth of such capital as the large amount of venture capital in the USA shows. In 1987, the American stock of venture capital exceeded US $30 billion, far surpassing Japan's US $2 billion and Germany's US $0.8 billion.[8] In countries where capital markets are not deep enough, the challenge facing governments is to create conditions for the provision of risk capital. These policies may range from tax policies, such as lowering capital-gains taxes and/or giving tax credits to R&D investments, to the establishment of financial institutions with the specific aim of providing risk capital. In Britain, lower income-tax rates coupled with direct government incentives, like the Business Expansion Scheme, have helped increase annual investment in venture capital 90-fold since 1979.[9] The establishment of venture-capital companies by governments in Germany and Japan in the early 1980s shows those governments' awareness of new developments in the world economy. The real obstacle in the development of venture capital in those countries may be their lack of entrepreneurial culture. This is the area where the USA's comparative advantage lies, and which is difficult to imitate by industrial policies.

COMPETING IN THE WORLD ECONOMY: FIRM BEHAVIOUR

Abegglen and Stalk (1985) analyse the way Japanese firms perceive the competitive process.[10] They have four basic perceptions about competing in world markets:

- market share is seen as the key indicator of performance (as suggested in Chapter 4);
- price becomes the principal competitive weapon to gain and hold the market share – cost reductions are passed to prices;
- investments in facilities are increased at least as high as the growth rate of the market and usually at a higher rate to maintain market shares in high-growth markets; and
- continuous technological innovation is crucial to maintain cost and price efficiency at all times in order to continue to hold and increase their market shares.

The market-share objective and innovative behaviour of Japanese firms competing in world markets fit the survival process described in earlier chapters exactly. As the world product and financial markets integrate, the innovative behaviour of Japanese firms accelerates, as Abegglen and Stalk (1985) note. When 1975 is taken as the base year for real increases in research expenditures, Japanese research expenditures increased from 100 in 1975, to 130 in 1980 and to 152 in 1982. The numbers for the USA for the same period were 100, 125 and 128.

Inoue (1989) emphasizes the changing financial structure of Japanese firms. He points out three characteristics:

- The inhibition of obtaining external funds and increased dependence on internal financing. This is indicated by the increase in the ratio of net worth to total assets of large corporations from 14 per cent to 23.9 per cent in the decade between 1976 and 1986, as seen from Table 7.2.
- The shift from loans to capital-market instruments. The ratio of loans and discount bills to total funds declined from 41.7 per cent in 1976 to 34.2 per cent in 1986. During the same time period, the ratio of corporate bonds and equity increased from 10.8 per cent to 15.3 per cent (Table 7.2).
- The diversification in the means of external financing. While the share of Yen-denominated loans declined, the share of corporate bonds and equities increased, including

*Table 7.2   Sources of funds by large firms, all industry in Japan
              (per cent of total capital)*

Sources of funds	1976	1981	1986
Accounts payable	21.2	20.8	15.2
Discount bills	5.3	4.8	2.3
Short-term loans (financial institutions)	16.3	16.1	17.9
Long-term loans (financial institutions)	20.1	16.5	14.0
	(41.7)	(37.4)	(34.2)
Bonds	4.4	5.0	8.6
Net worth	14.0	17.7	23.9
Capital	6.4	6.0	6.7
Surplus	7.6	11.8	17.2

Source: Inoue 1989, Table 2.

more emphasis on foreign-currency denominated bonds.
With the internationalization of financial markets, Japanese firms started to take advantage of the world capital
markets rather than limiting themselves to national ones.
Hodder (1988) also concludes that the increase in potential lenders, especially in the number of foreign lenders,
makes it much more difficult for the main bank to control
actions of client firms in Japan. The weakening of the
main bank control through financial deregulation is associated with a greater dependence on internal firms.

Japanese firms have been operating increasingly in the
securities-based world financial system initiated by the internationalization of financial markets. They have changed their
behaviour accordingly in conformity with the predictions of
firm behaviour based on the survival-process framework. As
was discussed (see pp. 160–69), such a framework also permits
the evaluation of government policies with respect to the
survival struggle in the world economy.

NOTES

1. See Scott and Lodge (eds) (1985), Krugman (ed.) (1986).
2. The following sections draw from Capoglu (1990).
3. For a survey see Norton (1986).
4. For example, see Carrington and Edwards (1981), and for similar comments Harris *et al.* (eds) (1988: 343–7.) For an analysis of credit-versus securities-based financial systems at a macro level, see Zysman (1983).
5. Suzuki (1986) provides an excellent account of money, finance and macroeconomic performance in Japan.
6. See Blumenthal (1988) and Malmgren (1988).
7. For similar arguments, see Drucker (1987), Okimoto (1986: 541–68) and the *Wall Street Journal*, 'Japan's Troubled Industries Stress R&D', 25 March 1987: 28.
8. *Financial Times*, 'Survey of Venture Capital, 30 November 1988.
9. *Economist*, 'Euroventure Capital Pepperoni and Chips', 4 June 1988: 84–5.
10. Abegglen and Stalk (1985: 34).
11. Abegglen and Stalk (1985: 125), Table 6.4.

8. Conclusions

This study has developed a concept of competition based on the survival process in capitalist economies. The conceptual framework suggested in this study has been operationalized through a model and tested econometrically. The basic features of the conceptual framework are as follows:

- Firms' desire to make profits requires the ability to make profits through the collective interaction of firms. This is the basic condition of survival as understood in this study.
- Uncertainty about the future and rivals' behaviour make investment and technological change the two most important aspects of competition.
- Competition in investment influences the pricing and financing behaviour of firms. Firms' profit targets are determined by their investment decisions.
- The nature of competition is determined by the institutional structure of the economy. Financial markets, by determining the availability and conditions of capital, affect firm behaviour.

It is argued that static criteria used in measuring the competitive behaviour and profitability of firms, such as concentration ratios and profit margins, are misleading and should be abandoned by the approaches that perceive competition as a dynamic process. It is suggested that the ratio of research and development expenditures to investment expenditures ($R\&D/I$) provides a better measure of competitive behaviour of firms in a dynamic sense as characterized by the survival process. In a similar fashion, the ratio of internal funds to investment expenditures (IF/I) is a dynamic profitability measure that overcomes the problems associated with the static measure of profit margins.

There are three empirically testable hypotheses that can be derived from the model based on the conceptual framework proposed in this study.

- Firms' pricing behaviour can be described as profit targeting. Firms' profit targets are determined by their investment decisions. Prices are set up so as to include the targeted profits over costs on the basis of firms' output expectations. Profit-targeting behaviour was tested for ten SIC two-digit manufacturing industries by constructing a price variable on the basis of profit-targeting behaviour. The empirical results strongly support such behaviour.
- Structural variables are significant in explaining the variations in internal financing ratios across industries and within an industry over a time period. These structural determinants are import competition, capital intensity, technological dynamics and the growth rate of output, and their significance was indicated by the time-series and cross-section analyses. Empirical results show that the capital availability for modernization purposes is available for most industries in the USA. However, the availability of risk capital for financing *R&D* expenditures is limited. Firms are constrained with their internal funds in financing risky technological innovations.
- Firm behaviour is affected by the institutional structure of the financial markets. This hypothesis is evaluated from a comparative perspective and tested statistically in the international context. The differences in the financial structures of firms across the USA, Japan and Germany are embodied in the financial systems of these countries. The importance of those systems is also reflected in the differences in the concentration ratios and the technological dynamics of firms in different countries. In the securities-based system of the USA, where investable funds are readily available to profitable firms, the concentration ratios are lower relative to the credit-based systems of Japan and Germany where the close relationships between

the incumbent firms and banks restrict the availability of capital to potential entrants. In the USA, the relative ready availability of capital to potential entrants puts pressure on incumbent firms to innovate continuously in order to stay competitive. This is reflected in the much higher ratio of *R&D* expenditures in the USA relative to Japan and Germany. These results are generalized in a statistical analysis for the OECD countries for which data are available. Accordingly, the institutional structures of the financial systems existing in these countries can explain a large part of the variations in the financing patterns and technological dynamics across these countries.

Finally, the recent dynamics of the world economy as reflected in the internationalization of financial markets and the changing nature of competitiveness were reviewed to argue that the conceptual framework presented in this study easily integrates these developments and predicts the changes in firm behaviour resulting from these dynamics. The case of Japanese firms was used to show that the trend of increasing dependence on internal funds by Japanese firms can be predicted from the survival model as the environment in which firms operate changes from a credit-based to a securities-based financial system. This also implies an increase in pressure to innovate as evidenced by the increasing *R&D* expenditures of Japanese firms.

RESEARCH AGENDA

This study is based on the central role of competition in economic theory and suggested a conception of competition as a survival process. The emphasis was on the conceptualization, operationalization and testing of this concept. Several research topics were raised which could not be answered within the scope of the study. These research topics are direct outcomes of this conception of competition. The extent of other research topics will show the fruitfulness of the idea of competition as a survival process.

One important topic is related to the macroeconomic considerations in firms' pricing decisions. It was argued in Chapter 4 that if firms' profit targets are not met, two situations are possible: total profits in the economy are enough to justify the planned investment needs of firms, but relative prices are not formed in a way that distributes the total profits in accordance with sectoral needs; and total profits in the economy are not enough to justify the planned investment needs. In the first case, a correction in relative prices is needed which may be brought about through price changes, entry and technological changes that save on inputs which have become expensive, or intensified intra-industry competition that shifts market share and may increase concentration. In the second case, if total profits are not enough to meet total investment needs, an inflationary spiral may result due to firms' efforts to capture higher shares of total profits by raising prices. It should be noted that the source of inflation mentioned here adds another dimension to the post-Keynesian inflation models. In those models, inflation results from a distributional conflict between firms and workers. In the analysis suggested in Chapter 4, inflation may result from a competitive struggle which involves firms and industries. The development of such an analysis is very useful for a theory of inflation and will help to clarify the macroeconomic constraints on firm behaviour and distributional issues.

At the micro level, the analyses of firms' investment behaviour have not been researched at a desirable level. The role of the competitive process especially needs to be integrated into empirical models of investment behaviour. Such models will improve our understanding of the investment process in the economy and will enrich our theoretical formulations which occupy a very important place in post-Keynesian theory.

A final point is on the issue of the methodological diversity in post-Keynesian economics. The disadvantages of the methodological diversity in post-Keynesian economics have been recently discussed by Caldwell (1989). The disadvantages he mentions range from the inconsistencies between different methodological positions of post-Keynesians to the binding theme of opposition to neoclassical economic theory. Efforts to achieve methodological unity will not only overcome these disadvantages but will also lead to the advancement of the post-Keynesian approach as a strong alternative paradigm in economics. The development of a theoretical approach is possible if the unifying methodology is refined by adherents through continuous research and self-criticism.

An important reason for the lack of such methodological unity has been the absence of a post-Keynesian competition theory. This has led post-Keynesians, who essentially perceive competition as a process, to associate themselves with schools, ranging from Marxists to Austrians, which focus on class struggle or individuals respectively as the leading dynamics of the competitive process. As reviewed in Chapter 2, a considerable number of writers in the post-Keynesian tradition, from Kalecki to Eichner, have adopted the imperfect-competition strand of neoclassical competition theory. This has prevented the development of a post-Keynesian conception of competition. At the same time, the post-Keynesians have missed the opportunity to benefit from the unifying nature of the concept of competition, the single most important organizing concept in economic theory as shown in the development of neoclassical and Marxian theories. The author hopes that the suggestion of the conception of competition as a survival process in this study will stimulate the development of a concept of competition particular to post-Keynesians.

References

Abegglen, J.C. and Stalk, G. (1985), *Kaisha, The Japanese Corporation* (Basic Books: New York).

Alchian, A.A. (1950), 'Uncertainty, Evolution and Economic Theory', *Journal of Political Economy*, Vol. LVIII.

Anderson, W.H.L. (1964), *Corporate Finance and Fixed Investment: An Econometric Study* (Harvard University Press: Boston).

Ando, A. (1975), 'Some Aspects of Stabilization Policies: The Monetarist Controversy and the MPS Model', in L. Klein *et al. Econometric Model Performance* (University of Pennsylvania Press: Philadelphia).

Andrews, P.W.S. (1964), *On Competition in Economic Theory* (Macmillan: London).

_____ and Brunner, E. (1975), *Studies in Pricing* (Macmillan: London).

Arestis, P. (1989), 'Pricing, Distribution, Investment and Growth: The Economics of A.S. Eichner', *Review of Political Economy*, Vol. 1, No. 1 (March).

_____ and Kitromilides, Y. (ed.) (1990) *Theory and Policy in Political Economy* (Edward Elgar: Aldershot).

Arrow, K.J. and Hahn, F.H. (1971), *General Competitive Analysis* (Holden-Day: San Francisco).

Auerbach, A.J. (1985), 'Real Determinants of Corporate Leverage in the United States', in B. Friedman, *Corporate Capital Structures in the US* (University of Chicago Press: Chicago).

Auerbach, P. (1988), *Competition, The Economics of Industrial Change* (Basil Blackwell: Oxford).

Baden-Fuller, C.W.F. (1989), 'Exit from Declining Industries and the Case of Steel Castings', *Economic Journal*, Vol. 99

(December).

Bain, J.S. (1956), *Barriers to New Competition* (Harvard University Press: Cambridge, MA).

Baran, P. and Sweezy, P. (1966), *Monopoly Capital* (Monthly Review Press: New York).

Barroux, Y. (1988), 'Comments', *European Economic Review*, Vol. 32 (June).

Baumol, W.J.L., Panzar, J.C. and Willig, R.D. (1982) *Contestable Markets and Theory of Industry Structure* (Harcourt, Brace, Jovanich: New York).

Baumol, W.J.L. *et al.* (1973), 'Efficiency of Corporate Investment: Reply', *Review of Economics and Statistics*, Vol. 55.

Baumol, W.J.L. *et al.* (1970), 'Earnings Retention, New Capital, and the Growth of the Firm', *Review of Economics and Statistics*, Vol. 52.

Baylis, B.T. and Buttphilip, A.A.S. (1980), *Capital Markets and Industrial Investment in Germany and France* (Saxon House Press: London).

Blumenthal, W.M. (1988), 'The World Economy and Technological Change', *Foreign Affairs*, Vol. 66, No. 3.

Brenner, R. (1987), *Rivalry in Business Science Among Nations* (Cambridge University Press: Cambridge).

Brittain, J.A. (1964), 'The Tax structure and Corporate Dividend Policy', *American Economic Review*.

_____ (1966), *Corporate Dividend Policy* (Brookings Institution: Washington DC).

Bronte, S. (1982), *Japanese Financial Markets and Institutions* (Euromoney Publications: London).

Byran, R. (1985), 'Monopoly in Marxist Method', *Capital and Class*, No. 26.

Cable, J.R. (1985), 'The Bank–Industry Relationship in West Germany: Performance on Policy Aspects', in J. Schwalback *Industry Structure and Performance*.

Caldwell, B.J. (1989), 'Post-Keynesian Methodology: An Assessment', *Review of Political Economy*, Vol. 1, No. 1 (March).

Cameron, R. (ed.) (1972), *Banking and Economic Development: Some Lessons of History* (Oxford University Press: New York).

Capoglu, G. (1987), Prices, Profits, and Financial Structures: A Post-Keynesian Approach, PhD dissertation, University of California, Berkeley.

———— (1990), 'The Internationalization of Financial Markets and Competitiveness in World Economy', *Journal of World Trade* Vol. 24, No. 2 (April).

Carrington, J.C. and Edwards, G.T. (1981), *Reversing Economic Decline* (St Martin's Press: New York).

Caves, R. and Uekusa, M. (1976), 'Industrial Organization', in H. Patrick (ed.) *Asia's New Giant.*

Chamberlain, E.H. (1933), *The Theory of Monopolistic Competition*, (Harvard University Press: Cambridge).

Clark, J.M. (1940), 'Towards A Concept of Workable Competition', *American Economic Review*, Vol. 30.

———— (1955), 'Competition: Static Models and Dynamic Aspects', *American Economic Review*, Vol. 45.

———— (1961), *Competition as a Dynamic Process* (Brookings Institution: Washington DC).

Clark, P.K. (1979), 'Investment in the 1970s: Theory, Performance and Prediction', *Brookings Papers on Economic Activity* (1).

Clifton, J.A. (1977), 'Competition and the Evolution of the Capitalist Mode of Production', *Cambridge Journal of Economics*, Vol. 1.

Coutts, K., Godley, W. and Nordhaus, W. (1978), *Industrial Prices in the United Kingdom* (Cambridge University Press: Cambridge).

Cowling, K. (1982), *Monopoly Capitalism* (John Wiley and Sons: New York).

Crane, D., Kimball, R. and Gregor, W. (1983), *The Effects of Banking Deregulation*, Association of Reserve City Bankers.

Creamer, D., Dobrovolsky, S. and Borenstein, I. (1960), *Capital in Manufacturing and Mining: Its Formation and Financing* (Princeton University Press: Princeton).

Cyert, R.M. and March, J.G. (1963), *A Behavioral Theory of the Firm* (Prentice-Hall: Englewood Cliffs).

Davies, J.E. and Lee, S.L. (1988), 'A Post-Keynesian Appraisal of the Contestability Criterion', *Journal of Post-Keynesian Economics*, Vol. 11.

Dennis, K.G. (1977), *Competition in the History of Economic Thought* (Arno Press: New York).

Dobb, M. (1973), *Theories of Value and Distribution Since Adam Smith* (Cambridge University Press: Cambridge).

Dougherty, C. (1980), *Interest and Profit* (Columbia University Press: New York).

Downie, J. (1958), *The Competitive Process* (Gerald Duckworth Press: London).

Drucker, P. (1987), 'Japan's Choices', *Foreign Affairs*, Vol. 65, No. 5.

Duesenberry, J.S. (1958), *Business Cycles and Economic Growth* (McGraw Hill: New York).

Dumenil, G. and Levy, D. (1987), 'The Dynamics of Competition: A Restoration of the Classical Analysis', *Cambridge Journal of Economics*, Vol. 11, No. 2 (June).

Eatwell, J. and Milgate, M. (eds) (1983), *Keynes's Economics and the Theory of Value and Distribution* (Duckworth: London).

Eckstein, O. (1984), *The DRI Report on US Manufacturing Industries* (McGraw Hill: New York).

Eckstein, W. (1980), 'The Role of Banks in Corporate Concentration in West Germany', *Zeitschrift Fur die Gesamte Staatwissenschaft* Vol. 136, No. 3 (September).

Edwards, J. (1987), 'Recent Developments in Theory of Corporate Finance', *Oxford Review of Economic Policy* (Winter).

Eichner, A.S. (1976), *The Megacorp and Oligopoly: Micro Foundations of Macro Dynamics* (Cambridge University Press: Cambridge).

_____ (1979), *A Guide to Post-Keynesian Economics* (M.S. Sharpe: White Plains).

Farjoun, E. and Machover, M. (1983), *Laws of Chaos: A Probabilistic Approach to Political Economy* (Verso: London).

Feldman, R.A. (1986), *Japanese Financial Markets* (MIT Press: Cambridge, MA).

Fine, B. and Murfin, A. (1984). *Macroeconomics and Monopoly Capitalism* (St Martin's Press: New York).

Fox, M.B. (1987), *Finance and Industrial Performance in Dynamic Economy* (Columbia University Press: New York).

Francke, H. and Hudson, M. (1986), *Banking and Finance in West Germany* (Croom Helm: London).

Friedman, B.M. (1980), 'Postwar Changes in the American Financial Markets', in Feldstein, M. (ed.) *The American Economy in Transition* (University of Chicago Press: Chicago).

―――― (1982), *The Changing Roles of Debt and Equity in Financing US Capital Formation* (University of Chicago Press: Chicago).

Friedman, M. (1953), 'The Methodology of Positive Economics', in *Essays in Positive Economics* (Chicago University Press: Chicago).

Gaskins, D.W. (1971), 'Dynamic Limit Pricing: Optimal Pricing under Threat of Entry', *Journal of Economic Theory*, Vol. 3.

Geroski, P.A. (1987), 'Do Dominant Firms Decline?', in Hay, D. and Vickers, J. (ed.) *The Economics of Market Dominance* (Basil Blackwell: Oxford).

Gershenkron, A. (1962), *Economic Backwardness in Historical Perspective* (Harvard University Press: Cambridge, MA).

Gupta, S. (1988), 'Profits, Investment and Causality: An Examination of Alternative Paradigms', *Southern Economic Journal*, Vol. 55, No. 1 (July).

Harcourt, G.C. (1980), 'Discussion', *American Economic Review*, Vol. 70.

―――― and Kenyon, P. (1976), 'Pricing and Investment Decision', *Kyklos*.

Harris, D.J. (1978), *Capital Accumulation and Income Distribution* (Stanford University Press: Stanford).

Harris, L. *et al.* (eds) (1988), *New Perspectives on the Financial System* (Croom Helm: London).

Hayek, F. (1948), 'The Meaning of Competition', in Hayek, F. *Individualism and Economic Order* (University of Chicago Press: Chicago).

Hayes, S., Spence, M. and Marks, D. (1982), *Competition in the Investment Banking Industry* (Harvard University Press: Cambridge, MA).

Hennings, H. (1981), 'The Structure of Banking in West Germany', in *The British and German Banking System: A Com-*

parative Study, Economist's Advisory Group Ltd.

Hodder, J.E. (1988), 'Corporate Capital Structure in the United States and Japan: Financial Intermediation and Implications of Financial Deregulation', in Shoven, J. (ed.) *Government Policy Towards Industry in the United States and Japan* (Cambridge University Press: Cambridge).

Holland, M.H. (1984), *Measuring Profitability and Capital Costs* (Lexington Books: Lexington).

Houthakker, H.S. (1979), 'Growth and Inflation: Analysis by Industry', *Brookings Paper on Economic Activity*, No. 1.

Hu, Y. (1975), 'National Attitudes and the Financing of Industry', *Political and Economic Planning (PEP)*, Vol. XLI, No. 559 (December).

Inoue, Y. (1989), 'Globalization of Business Finance', *Japanese Economic Studies*, Vol. 17, No. 4 (Summer).

Jorgenson, D.W. (1963), 'Capital Theory and Investment Behavior', *American Economic Review Proceedings*, Vol. 53 (May).

_____ (1971), 'Econometric Studies of Investment Behavior: A Survey', *Journal of Economic Literature*, Vol. 6.

Kalecki, M. (1937), 'The Principle of Increasing Risk', *Economica*, Vol. 4.

_____ (1971), *Selected Essays on the Dynamics of the Capitalist Economy, 1933–1970* (Cambridge University Press: Cambridge).

Kenyon, P. (1979), 'Pricing', in Eichner, A. *A Guide to Post-Keynesian Economics*.

_____ (1980), 'Discussion', *American Economic Review*, Vol. 70.

Keynes, J.M. (1936), *The General Theory of Employment, Interest and Money* (Macmillan: London).

Kirzner, I.M. (1973), *Competition and Entrepreneurship* (University of Chicago Press: Chicago).

Klein, B.H. (1977), *Dynamic Economics* (Harvard University Press: Cambridge, MA).

Knight, F. (1921), *Risk, Uncertainty and Profit* (Houghton Mifflin Company: Boston).

Koopmans, T.C. (1957), *Three Essays on the State of Economic Science* (McGraw-Hill: New York).

Koutsoyiannis, A. (1984), 'Goals of Oligopolistic Firms', *Southern Economic Journal* (December).

Kreps, D. and Spence, A.M. (1983), 'Modelling the Role of History in Industrial Organization and Competition', forthcoming in Feiwell, G., *Contemporary Issues in Modern Microeconomics*.

Krugman, P. (ed.) (1986), *Strategic Trade Policy and the New International Economics* (MIT Press: Cambridge).

Kuhn, T.S. (1970), *The Structure of Scientific Revolutions* (Chicago University Press: Chicago).

Langlois, R.N. (ed.) (1986) *Economics as Process* (Cambridge University Press: Cambridge).

Lee, F.S. (1984), 'New Wine in a New Bottle', *Australian Economic Papers* (June).

_____ *et al.* (1986), 'P.W.S. Andrews' Theory of Competitive Oligopoly: A New Interpretation', *British Review of Economic Issues*, Vol. 8, No. 19 (Autumn).

Levine, D.P. (1981), *Economic Theory* Vol. II (Routledge & Kegan Paul: London).

Lintner, J. (1956), 'Distribution of Incomes of Corporations Among Dividends, Retained Earnings, and Taxes', *American Economic Review*.

Malmgren, H.B. (1988), 'Technological Challenges to Economic Policies', *Economic Impact*, Vol. 62.

Mankiw, G.N. (1988) 'Comments', *European Economic Review*, Vol. 32 (June).

Marglin, S.A. and Bhaduri, A. (1986), 'Distribution, Capacity Utilization, and Growth', unpublished paper.

Markham, J.W. (1950), 'An Alternative Approach to the Concept of Workable Competition', *American Economic Review*, Vol. XL.

Marx, K. (1967), *Capital*, Vols. I, III (International Publishers: New York).

Maycock, H. (1977), *European Banking* (Graham Trotman Limited: London).

Mayer, C. (1987), 'The Assessment: Financial Systems and Corporate Investment', *Oxford Review of Economic Policy*, Vol. 3 (Winter).

_____ (1988), 'New Issues in Corporate Finance', *European*

Economic Review, Vol. 32 (June).

McNulty, P. (1968), 'Economic Theory and the Meaning of Competition', *Quarterly Journal of Economics* (82).

Means, G.C. (1936), 'Notes on Flexible Prices', *American Economic Review*, Vol. 26.

Modigliani, F. (1958), 'New Developments in Oligopoly Front', *Journal of Political Economy*, Vol. 66.

_____ and Miller, M. (1958), 'The Cost of Capital, Corporation Finance and the Theory of Investment', *American Economic Review* (June).

Mueller, D.C. (1986), *Profits in the Long Run* (Cambridge University Press: Cambridge).

Nakatani, I. (1986), 'Towards the New International Economic Order – The Role of Japan in the World Economy', *Hitotsubashi Journal of Economics*, Vol. 27.

Nelson, R.R. and Winter, S.G. (1982), *An Evolutionary Theory of Economic Change* (Belknap Press of Harvard University Press: Cambridge, MA).

Nikaido, H. (1983), 'Marx on Competition', *Zeitschrift fur Nationalekonomie*, Vol. 43.

Norton, R.D. (1986), 'Industrial Policy and American Renewal', *Journal of Economic Literature*, March.

O'Driscoll, G. and Rizzo, M.J. (1985), *The Economics of Time and Ignorance* (Basil Blackwell: Oxford).

Obrinsky, M. (1983), *Profit Theory and Capitalism* (University of Philadelphia Press: Philadelphia).

Okimoto, D.I. (1986), 'The Japanese Challenge in High Technology', in Landau, R. and Rosenberg, N. (eds) *The Positive Sum Strategy* (National Academy Press: Washington DC).

Ong, N. (1981), 'Target Pricing, Competition and Growth', *Journal of Post-Keynesian Economics*, Vol. 4, No. 1 (Fall).

Pindyck, R. and Rubinfield, D. (1981), *Econometric Models and Econometric Forecasts* (McGraw Hill, Inc.: New York).

Pollin, R. (1983), 'Alternative Perspectives on the Rise of Corporate Debt and Dependency: The US Post-War Experience', unpublished paper (UC Riverside).

Reid, G. (1987), *Theories of Industrial Organization* (Basil Blackwell: Oxford).

Reynolds, P. (1987), *Political Economy – A Synthesis of Kaleck-*

ian and Post-Keynesian Economics (Wheatsheaf Books: Sussex, St Martin's Press: New York).

———— (1990), 'Kaleckian and Post-Keynesian Theories of Pricing: Some Extensions and Implications', in Arestis, P. *Theory and Policy in Political Economy*.

Robinson, J. (1933), *The Economics of Imperfect Competition* (Macmillan: London).

———— (1971), *Economic Heresies* (Basis Books: New York).

Rutterford, J. (1988), 'An International Perspective on the Capital Structure Puzzle', in Stein, J. and Chew, D. (eds) *New Developments in International Finance* (Basil Blackwell: New York).

Sakakibara, *et al.* (1982), *Japanese Financial System in Comparative Perspective* (US Congress Joint Economic Committee: Washington, DC).

Samuels, J.M., Groves, R. and Goddard, C.S. (1975), *Company Finance in Europe* (Unwin Brothers: London).

Sawyer, M.C. (1979), *Theories of the Firm* (St Martin's Press: New York).

———— (1983), *Business Pricing and Inflation* (The Macmillan Press: London).

———— (1985), *The Economics of Michal Kalecki* (Macmillan: London).

———— (1990), 'On the Post-Keynesian Tradition and Industrial Economics', *Review of Political Economy*, Vol. 2, No. 1.

———— (ed.) (1988), *Post-Keynesian Economics* (Edward Elgar: Aldershot).

Scharfstein, D.S. and Stein, J.C. (1990), 'Herd Behavior and Investment', *American Economic Review*, Vol. 80, No. 3 (June).

Scherer, F.M. (1980), *Industrial Market Structure and Economic Performance* (Rand McNally: Chicago).

Schumpeter, J.A. (1934), 'Review of Robinson's Economics of Imperfect Competition', *Journal of Political Economy* (April).

———— (1942), *Capitalism, Socialism and Democracy* (Harper Publisher: New York).

Schwartz, M. and Reynolds, R.J. (1983), 'Contestable Markets: An Uprising in the Theory of Industry Structure: Comment',

American Economic Review, Vol. 73.

Scott, B.R. and Lodge, G.C. (eds) (1985), *US Competitiveness in the World Economy* (Harvard Business School Press: Boston).

Semmler, W. (1984a), *Competition, Monopoly and Differential Profit Rates* (Columbia University Press: New York).

———— (1984b), 'On the Classical Theory of Competition, Value and Prices of Production', Australian Economic Papers, (June).

Shaik, A. (1978), 'Political Economy and Capitalism: Notes on Dobb's Theory of Crisis', *Cambridge Journal of Economics*, Vol. 2.

Shapiro, N. (1981), 'Pricing and Growth of Firms', *Journal of Post-Keynesian Economics*, Vol. 4, No. 1 (Fall).

Shepherd, W.G. (1984), 'Contestability vs. Competition', *American Economic Review*, Vol. 74.

Smith, A. (1970). *An Inquiry into the Nature and Causes of the Wealth of Nations* (Penguin Books: New York).

Smith, R.K. (1969), 'The Effect of Uncertainty on Monopoly Price, Capital Stock and Utilization of Capital', *Journal of Economic Theory*, No. 1.

Solow, R. (1957), 'Technical Change and the Aggregate Production Function', *Review of Economics and Statistics*, Vol. 39.

Spence, M. (1985), 'Capital Structure and the Corporation's Product Market Environment', in *Corporate Capital Structures in the US*, Friedman, B. (ed.) (University of Chicago Press: Chicago).

Steindl, J. (1976), *Maturity and Stagnation in American Capitalism* (Monthly Review Press: New York).

Stigler, G.J. (1957), 'Perfect Competition, Historically Contemplated', in *Essays in the History of Economics* (University of Chicago Press: Chicago).

Suzuki, Y. (1980) *Money and Banking in Contemporary Japan* (Yale University Press: New Haven).

———— (1986), *Money, Finance and Macroeconomic Performance in Japan* (Yale University Press: New Haven).

Sylos-Labini, P. (1962), *Oligopoly and Technical Progress* (Harvard University Press: Cambridge, MA).

_____ (1979), 'Industrial Pricing in the UK', *Cambridge Journal of Economics* (June).

_____ (1984), *The Forces of Economic Growth and Decline* (MIT Press: Cambridge).

Taggart, R.A., (1984), *Have US Corporations Grown Financially Weak?* NBER Working Paper No. 1523.

Turnovsky, S.J. (1967), 'The Allocation of Corporate Profits Between Dividends and Retained Earnings', *Review of Economics and Statistics*.

Vickers, D. (1978), *Financial Markets in the Capitalist Process* (University of Pennsylvania Press: Philadelphia).

Vittas, D. (1978), *Banking Systems Abroad* (Interbank Research Organization: London).

Wallich, H. and Wallich, M. (1976), 'Banking and Finance', in Patrick, H. and Rosovsky, H. (eds) *Asia's New Giant: How the Japanese Economy Works* (Brookings Institution: Washington DC).

Walsh, V. and Gram, H. (1980), *Classical and Neoclassical Theories of General Equilibrium: Historical Origins and Mathematical Structure* (Oxford University Press: Oxford).

Ward, B.N. (1972), *What's Wrong with Economics* (Basic Books: New York).

_____ (1979), *The Ideal Worlds of Economics* (Basic Books: New York).

Weeks, J. (1981), *Capital and Exploitation* (Princeton University Press: Princeton).

Weintraub, E.R. (1980), *The Microfoundations of Macroeconomics* (Cambridge University Press: Cambridge).

Wellons, P. (1985), 'Competitiveness in the World Economy: The Role of the US Financial System', in Scott, B. (ed.) *US Competitiveness in the World Economy*.

Wood, A. (1975), *A Theory of Profits* (Cambridge University Press: Cambridge).

Zysman, J. (1983), *Governments, Markets and Growth* (Cornell University Press: Ithaca).

Index